Y0-AGK-892

Panasonic

Microwave Oven Cookbook

Microwave cooking is convenient, and time saving and versatile. Not only can it be used to warm leftovers, or prepare last-minute dinners, but also for leisurely breakfasts to elegant party menus.

This cookbook contains directions for cooking foods from appetizers to desserts to warming your bedtime milk. To be successful with microwave cooking, read the operating manual and introduction to the cookbook. Each chapter gives tips and techniques to help good results.

We have included some of our favorite recipes in this cookbook. After trying these recipes, we encourage you to experiment and adapt your favorites to microwave cooking. Use our recipes as a guide for cooking times and power levels, dish size and cooking technique. Relax and enjoy your new Panasonic microwave oven.

Sincerely,
Matsushita Appliance Co.

Please direct all inquiries to:

Matsushita Appliance Company
Division of Matsushita Electric Corporation of America
One Panasonic Way
Secaucus, New Jersey 07094
201-348-7000

In Canada:

PANASONIC HOME ECONOMIST
PANASONIC CANADA
Division of Matsushita Electric
of Canada Limited
5770 Ambler Drive
Mississauga, Ontario L4W2T3
(416) 624-5010

Table of Contents 1

Understanding how your microwave oven works and realizing the benefits over conventional cooking will reinforce your decision to become a microwave oven cook.

Having carefully reviewed the operating instructions, settle down with a cup of tea or coffee and read what cooking with this amazing unit is all about... and plan dinner for tonight.

COOKING WITH MICROWAVE ENERGY

Microwaves are a form of high frequency radio waves similar to those used by a radio including AM, FM, and CB. They are, however, much shorter than radio waves; approximately four to six inches long with a diameter of about one-fourth inch. Electricity is converted into microwave energy by the magnetron tube. From the magnetron tube, microwave energy is transmitted to the oven cavity where it is: reflected, transmitted and absorbed.

Reflection
Microwaves are reflected by metal just as a ball is bounced off a wall. A combination of stationary (interior walls) and rotating metal (turntable or stirrer fan) helps assure that the microwaves are well distributed within the oven cavity to produce even cooking.

Transmission
Microwaves pass through some materials such as paper, glass and plastic much like sunlight shining through a window.
Because these substances do not absorb or reflect the microwave energy, they are ideal materials for microwave oven cooking containers.

Absorption
During heating, microwaves will be absorbed by food. They penetrate to a depth of about $3/4$ to $1^1/2$ inches. Microwave energy excites the molecules in the food (especially water, fat and sugar molecules), and causes them to vibrate at a rate of 2,450,000,000 times per second. This vibration causes friction, and heat is produced. If you vigorously rub your hands together, you will feel heat produced by friction. The internal cooking of larger foods is done by conduction. The heat which is produced by friction is conducted to the center of the food. Foods also continue to cook by conduction during standing time (see page 10). Because microwaves dissipate, much like sunlight as it reaches the Earth's surface, they cannot be stored in food.

Reflection

Transmission

Absorption

COOKING EQUIPMENT

Microwave cooking opens new possibilities in convenience and flexibility for cooking containers. There are new microwave accessories constantly being introduced, but do not feel you need to purchase all new equipment. Many items you already have can be tested to see if they are microwave oven safe. You'll be surprised at the numerous things you already have in your kitchen that are suitable for microwave cooking.

Glass, Ceramic and China

Most of these utensils are excellent for use in the microwave oven. Many manufacturers now identify microwave oven safe dishes with either an asterisk (*) or a note in the accompanying product literature. Heat resistant glassware, unless it has metallic trim or decoration, can most always be used. However, be careful about using delicate glassware since it may crack, not from microwave energy, but from the heat of the food. The most well-known microwave oven safe glassware are Corning® products. Corning now marks its products "good for microwave" or "good for range and microwave." Corelle® Livingware (by Corning), with the exception of the closed handle cups, is microwave oven safe.
Pyrex® (by Corning) without metallic trim is microwave oven safe and has unique pieces in its line. Other glass utensils that are also microwave oven safe include: Fire-King® (by Anchor Hocking), Glassbake® (by Jeannette Glass), Glass Ovenware® (by Heller Designs) and oven ware by Federal Glass®.
Dinnerware such as Temperware® (by Lenox®) that is marked ovenproof is usually safe to use in the microwave oven. To check for microwave oven safety, do dish test on page 4.

With all these possibilities, just remember a few basic things...
DO NOT USE
- utensils with metallic trim or parts (i.e. bands, screws, etc.)
- dishware with cracked or crazed glazes
- ceramic mugs or cups with glued on handles
- delicate glassware

Here is a list of heat-resistant glass cookware we find invaluable in microwave cookery. You probably have many of these items on your shelf already:

- measuring cups
- custard cups
- mixing bowls
- loaf dish
- covered casserole dishes
- oblong baking dish
- cake dishes, round or square
- pie plate

WHEN IN DOUBT... DO THE SIMPLE DISH TEST

How to Test a Container for Safe Microwave Oven Use:

Fill a 1-cup glass measure with water and place it in the microwave oven along with the container to be tested; heat 1½ minutes at HIGH. If the container is microwave oven safe, it should remain comfortably cool and the water should be hot. If the container is hot, it has absorbed some microwave energy and should not be used. This test cannot be used for plastic containers.

JARS and BOTTLES can be used to heat foods providing any metal lids are removed from the glass container. This is only for heating food to serving temperature, i.e., reheating leftovers. Cooking cannot be done safely because most of these containers are not heat-resistant and during extended heating times, heat from the food would cause cracking or breaking.
Note: *Do not use narrow neck bottles for reheating. They may shatter.*

Plastics
Plastic dishes, cups, and some freezer containers may be used in the microwave oven. There are numerous type of plastic products available, so choose carefully; some can become soft, distorted or pitted from the heat of the food. "Dishwasher Safe" is a good sign that the container will also be microwave oven safe. Plastic dishes should not be used for cooking over an extended period of time or with foods having high fat or sugar content.
- Containers made from and labeled UDEL® (by Union Carbide) or Polysulfone plastic are very durable in microwave cooking.
- Freezette® (by Republic Molding) storage containers can be safely used in the microwave oven for reheating.
- Melamine dishes are NOT microwave oven safe.
- Tupperware® (by Tupperware Home Parties) is NOT recommended for microwave oven cooking.

COOKING BAGS designed to withstand boiling, freezing, or conventional heating are safe to use in the microwave oven. These bags should be prepared according to manufacturer's package directions. Pull bag up around food. Close cooking bag with the special nylon tie provided, (see picture) otherwise, use a piece of cotton string, or a strip cut from the open end of the bag. Be sure to make six 1/2-inch slits in top of bag to allow steam to escape. DO NOT use plastic or paper covered, wire twist-tie to close bag. They can act as an antenna and cause arcing (blue sparks). Wire twist-ties could ignite, thereby damaging the oven.
DO NOT COOK IN PLASTIC FOOD STORAGE BAGS. They are not heat resistant and may melt from the heat of the food.

PLASTIC WRAP such as SARAN WRAP™ (by Dow Chemical Co.) can be used to cover dishes in most recipes. Over an extended cooking time, some disfiguration of the wrap may occur. When using plastic wrap as a casserole dish cover, fold back a small section of plastic wrap from the edge of the dish to allow some steam to escape. When removing plastic wrap "covers," as well as any glass lid, be careful to remove it away from you to avoid steam burns. After cooking, loosen plastic but let dish stand covered.

Paper
For short cooking times and for foods with a low fat or water content, paper is a convenient container for the microwave oven. NAPKINS, WAX PAPER, PAPER TOWELS, PLATES, CUPS, FREEZER WRAP, and CARDBOARD all are handy utensils. Avoid wax coated paper goods. Foods that reach high temperatures can melt the wax. Wax paper, however, can be used effectively to prevent spatter when cooking. A special category of paper products is the new polyestercoated paperboard pans. These sturdy pans come in a variety of sizes and can be used for heating any food. They are suitable for freezer-to-microwave oven use and are disposable.
Paper is also used in microwave cooking to absorb fat and excess moisture. Cooking bacon on a paper plate, between layers of paper towels is a common example of this.
CAUTION: Recycled paper products may contain impurities which when combined with hot fat could cause sparking (arcing) or fires when used for cooking in the microwave oven.

BROWNING DISHES are used to sear chops, meat patties, steaks, etc. The dish is first preheated for several minutes in the microwave oven at HIGH. A special coating on the bottom of the dish absorbs the microwave energy and becomes very hot. When foods are added to dish, the result is a seared effect.

- Preheat dish according to directions accompanying accessory.
- If using oil or butter, add after preheating.
- Add food to be seared and cook according to recipe or personal preference.
- Use pot holders to remove dish from microwave oven.
- Clean in dishwasher or with hot, sudsy water. For burned-on food, use nonabrasive cleanser. A plastic mesh pad recommended for glassware can be used. Do not use steel wool soap pads.
- Do not use browning dish on conventional gas or electric surface units, in oven, or under broiler.
- Do not use browning dish with the temperature probe.
- Check information included with browning dish for detailed instructions and cooking chart.

Straw, Wicker and Wood

Straw and wicker baskets may be used in the microwave oven for short periods of time to warm rolls or bread. Large wooden utensils, such as bowls or cutting boards should NOT be used for prolonged heating as the microwave energy may cause the wood to become dry and brittle.

Metal

Metal containers or utensils, and those with metallic trim, should NOT be used in the microwave oven. Since microwave energy is reflected by metal, foods in metal containers will not cook evenly.

There is also the possibility of "arcing." This is a static discharge or blue sparks between gaps in the metal or between the metal and the interior of the oven. Arcing may cause damage to the oven walls. If arcing occurs, turn the unit off and transfer food to a non-metallic container. Although metal utensils must be avoided in microwave cooking, some metal can be helpful when used correctly.

ALUMINUM FOIL can be used safely if certain guidelines are followed. Because it reflects microwave energy, foil can be used to an advantage in some recipes. It can be used to prevent overcooking. Small pieces of foil are used to cover areas such as chicken wings, tips of roasts, or other thin parts that cook before the rest of the recipe is finished. Foil is used in these cases to slow or stop the cooking process and prevent overcooking.

FOIL LINED CONTAINERS, either cardboard or plastic, should NOT be used in the microwave oven. Foil lined milk cartons, frozen orange juice concentrate containers, or baking containers, included in some cake mixes are examples of things to be avoided.

FROZEN DINNER TRAYS can be used in the microwave oven, but results are only satisfactory if the container is no higher than 3/4-inch. In metal containers, all the heating takes place from the top; the metal container reflects the energy directed to the sides and bottom. See Heating Frozen Convenience Foods, page 99.

METAL SKEWERS can be used if there is a large amount of food in proportion to the amount of metal. Take care in the placement of the skewers to avoid arcing between the skewers or between the skewers and the sides of the oven. Wooden skewers are the best and can be easily purchased at your local market, grocery store, or in the housewares section of many department stores.

THERMOMETERS are available for use in microwave ovens. DO NOT USE CONVENTIONAL MERCURY TYPE CANDY OR MEAT THERMOMETERS in food while heating in the microwave oven.

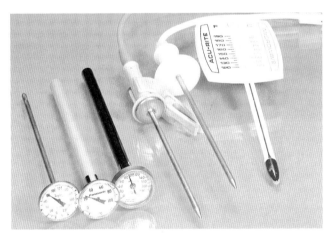

METAL TWIST-TIES either paper or plastic coated, should NOT be used in the microwave oven. See pictures and information under COOKING BAGS page 5.

PREPARING RECIPES AND COOKING TECHNIQUES

Ingredients
All ingredients are used as taken from their common storage place, unless otherwise indicated. For example, milk, eggs, and butter are used refrigerator cold. Recipes using canned ingredients include the liquid unless specified DRAINED. Other assumed things, unless clarified, are:
• flour is all-purpose
• milk is homogenized whole milk
• sugar is granulated white sugar (100% sucrose)
• eggs are large...Grade A
• amounts given are level measuring units (cup, teaspoon, etc.)

SPECIAL HINT: Pierce the skin or membrane of foods when cooked whole in the microwave oven. This allows steam to escape. Forgetting to do this creates the possibility of the food bursting when cooked with microwave energy. This is the main reason eggs cannot be hard boiled in their shell. The yolk and white membranes need to be pierced before cooking. The same technique is applied to fruits or vegetables with a skin when cooked whole (i.e., apples and potatoes).

Food Characteristics

Food characteristics which affect conventional cooking are more pronounced with microwave cooking.

Size and Quantity—Small portions cook faster than large ones.

Starting Temperatures—
Room temperature foods take less time to heat up than refrigerator or frozen foods.

Density—Porous, airy foods take less time to heat up than heavy, compact foods.

Bone and Fat—Both affect cooking. Bones conduct heat and cause the meat next to it to be heated more quickly. Large amounts of fat absorb microwave energy and meat next to these areas may overcook.

Shape—Uniform sizes cook more evenly. To compensate for irregular shapes, place thin pieces toward the center of the dish and thicker pieces toward the edge of dish.

Browning

Meats and poultry, cooked 10 to 15 minutes, brown from their own fat. Foods cooked for shorter periods of time can be aided with the help of a browning sauce, Worcestershire sauce, or soy sauce. Simply brush one of these sauces over meat or poultry before cooking. These sauces do not add or take away from the desired flavor of the recipe. Baked goods do not need long cooking time and, therefore, do not brown. When cakes or cupcakes will be frosted, no one will notice this visual difference. For quick breads or muffins, brown sugar can be used in the recipe in place of granulated sugar or the surface can be sprinkled with dark spices before baking.

Spacing

Individual foods, such as baked potatoes, cupcakes and hors d'oeuvres, will cook more evenly if placed in the oven equal distance apart. When possible, arrange foods in a circular pattern.

Similarly, when placing foods in a baking dish, arrange around the outside of dish, not lined up next to each other. Food should NOT be stacked on top of each other.

Covering

As with conventional cooking, moisture evaporates during microwave cooking. Because microwave cooking is done with time and not direct heat, the rate of evaporation cannot be as easily controlled. This, however, can be corrected by using different materials to cover dishes. Casserole lids or plastic wrap are used for a tighter seal. Various degrees of moisture retention are also obtained by using wax paper and paper towels.

Unless specified, a recipe is cooked uncovered. Cooking covered, refers to a casserole lid or plastic wrap. Other coverings are specified when necessary. When using plastic wrap for a cover, do not seal it tightly around the dish. A small amount of steam must be able to escape; leaving an area around the edge uncovered, meets this need.

Timing

A range in cooking time is given in each recipe for two reasons. First, to allow for the uncontrollable differences in food shapes, starting temperature and regional preferences. Secondly, to allow for the differences in electrical volt output power which changes during peak load periods. Always remember, it is easier to add time to an undercooked product. Once the food is overcooked, nothing can be done!

In each recipe an APPROXIMATE COOKING TIME is given. If a recipe is cooked in two "batches," the Approx. Time includes the extra cooking time.

Stirring

Stirring is usually necessary during microwave cooking. We have noted when stirring is helpful, using the words once, twice, frequently or occasionally to describe the amount of stirring necessary. Always bring the cooked outside edges toward the center and the less cooked center portions toward the outside.

Some foods should be turned in the container during heating. For example, because of the different thicknesses in the breast and back sections of poultry, a turkey is turned over once during cooking to insure more even cooking. Rearranging or turning food over in a dish should be done as indicated to insure a satisfactory end result.

Standing Time

Most foods will continue to cook by conduction after the microwave oven is turned off. In meat cookery, the internal temperature will rise 5°F to 15°F if allowed to stand, covered, for 10 to 15 minutes. Casseroles and vegetables need a shorter amount of standing time, but this standing time is necessary to allow foods to complete cooking in the center without overcooking on the edges.

Testing for Doneness

The same test for doneness used in conventional cooking may be used for microwave cooking.

Cakes are done when toothpick comes out clean and cake pulls away from side of the dish.

Meat is done when fork tender or splits at fibers.

Chicken is done when juices are clear yellow and drumstick moves freely.

Fish is done when it flakes and is opaque.

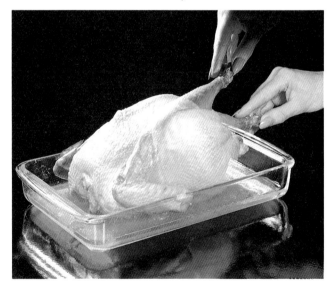

Reheating

Microwave reheating makes leftovers taste like they were freshly prepared. Below are general guidelines to follow when reheating various types of foods.

Baked Goods. Arrange 4 to 6 servings rolls, biscuits, etc. in a microwave safe serving container. Heat covered with paper napkin. Wrap a single roll in paper napkin and heat 1/4 to 1/2 minute.

Hint: Test baked goods before adding more heating time; when overheated these items become tough and hard.

Plates of Foods. Arrange foods on a microwave safe plate with thicker, denser portions towards the rim. Add gravy or butter where desired. Cover plate with wax paper.

Hint: Mashed potatoes will heat more evenly and quickly if spread out instead of mounded.

Casseroles. Stir in or add a small amount of liquid (water, milk, broth, gravy, etc.) and cover with a glass lid or plastic wrap. For casseroles with crumb-type toppings, cover with wax paper. Stir halfway through heating.

Sandwiches. Wrap closed sandwiches in paper towel. Place open-faced sandwiches on paper plate and cover with wax paper.

Converting Favorite Conventional Recipes

A basic rule, when converting conventional recipes to microwave recipes, is to cut the suggested cooking time to one-fourth. Also, find a similar microwave recipe and adapt that time and power setting.

Season meats with herbs and spices before cooking; salt after cooking. Since meat is not browned before cooking, omit any oil or fat that would have been used for browning. Reduce liquids by one-fourth. Cut meat for stewing into 1 to 1 1/2-inch pieces. Shield unevenly shaped meat.

Ingredients for casseroles should be cut to uniform sizes. Condensed cream soup makes a good base for casseroles. Stir during heating. Sprinkle crumb toppings on before stand time to keep them crisp.

DEFROSTING

Defrosting frozen foods is one of the benefits of having a microwave oven. Never again will you be caught with a freezer fully stocked with a wide variety of foods, but without enough time to defrost and prepare them for your family or unexpected company.

PREPARING MEAT FOR FREEZING

The finished quality of the prepared food will depend on the original quality before freezing, the care the food receives during freezing, and the techniques and times used for defrosting. Select good quality and fresh meat, poultry, or fish for freezing. Foods should be frozen as soon as possible after purchasing to preserve their quality. How foods are wrapped for freezing and the temperature they are frozen at, affect defrosting results. Proper wrapping materials should be used, and packaging techniques should be followed for best results.

WRAPPING MATERIALS best suited for use in the freezer are odorless, and moisture and vapor proof. Meats need to be removed from their wrappings before defrosting. Therefore, containers such as glass freezer jars and plastic freezer containers are unsuitable. Heavy-duty plastic wraps and bags, and freezer wrap are suitable.

Meats may also be frozen in their store packaging for short periods of time. (Note: If aluminum foil is used for wrapping, all pieces of foil should be removed before defrosting in your microwave oven. If small pieces adhere to frozen meat, arcing may occur.

When WRAPPING FOR FREEZING, arrange meat in thin uniform layers. Package ground meat in 1 to 2 inch thick rectangular, square or round shapes. Chicken pieces, chops and stew meat will defrost more easily if frozen in 1 or 2 piece layers rather than in bulky, thick packages. To aid in separating chops and hamburger patties during defrosting, place a piece of wax paper between the layers.

Remove giblets from fresh whole poultry. (The giblets may be frozen separately, if desired.) Clean and dry poultry. Tie legs and wings with string; this helps poultry keep its shape during freezing. If poultry is packaged frozen, it may be defrosted even though the giblets are inside the cavity. However, the cavity will be very icy after the defrosting cycle. It will be necessary to run cold water over the poulty.

Fish and seafoods are best frozen in single layers. Fillets may be frozen 2 or 3 deep, but place a piece of wax paper or plastic wrap between each layer. Shrimp or scallops may be quick frozen on a cookie sheet covered with plastic wrap. Once they are frozen, simply remove from the cookie sheet and place in a freezer bag or container. If they are thoroughly frozen before placing in the bag, they will not stick to each other.

Remove all air before sealing plastic bags. The drug store wrap is a good wrapping procedure to follow when using sheets of wrap such as freezer or plastic wrap. Center food to be wrapped on material. Bring two edges, up over the center and start folding down in 1 inch tucks until wrap is close to meat. Remove excess air from package. Shape ends into triangles and fold up over center. Tape securely.

LABEL package with type and cut of meat, date and weight.

FREEZE foods in a freezer which is maintained at 0°F or lower. Defrosting times given in the charts are for thoroughly frozen foods. (i.e. foods should be frozen at least 24 hours before defrosting.)

CYCLIC DEFROST

To use, touch the DEFROST pad and program defrosting time. The oven will automatically divide the defrost time into eight stages: 4 defrost and 4 stand periods. During the programmed time, the oven will alternate between defrost power and stand times (no power). Times for defrosting are in the Meat, Poultry, and Fish Chapters and Appendix.

PRECAUTIONS TO AVOID POSSIBLE EXPOSURE TO EXCESSIVE MICROWAVE ENERGY

(a) **Do not attempt to operate this oven with the door open** since open-door operation can result in harmful exposure to microwave energy. It is important not to defeat or tamper with the safety interlocks.

(b) **Do not place any object** between the oven front face and the door or allow soil or cleaner residue to accumulate on sealing surfaces.

(c) **Do not operate the oven** if it is damaged. It is particularly important that the oven door close properly and that there is no damage to the:
    (1) door (bent)
    (2) hinges and latches (broken or loosened)
    (3) door seals and sealing surfaces

(d) **The oven should not be adjusted or repaired** by anyone except properly qualified service personnel.

BEFORE CALLING FOR SERVICE

Many times a service call can be avoided by checking a few simple things. The following conditions are not caused by a defect in the unit itself, so please check the following points before requesting service.

Condition	Time-Saving Checks
No Power	★ Oven plugged in? ★ Check home fuse or circuit breaker.
Oven not operating	★ Oven door closed? ★ Controls set properly?
Takes longer than time in cookbook	★ Incorrect power selection? ★ Low voltage at power outlet? ★ Starting temp. and shape of foods vary, so simply cook a little longer.
Uneven cooking Undercooking or Overcooking	★ Improperly wrapped or used incorrect container? ★ Controls set properly? ★ For large meat, utilize standing time at room temperature after cooking.
Oven light flickers	★ This is normal.
Water condensation around door	★ This is normal—merely wipe dry.
Sparks occur	★ Metallic wrap or container touching oven wall. ★ Dish or glassware trimmed in gold or silver. ★ Container has metal parts or trim.

PANASONIC RECOMMENDS THE FOLLOWING REGARDING COOKING SPECIFIC FOODS IN YOUR MICROWAVE OVEN:

1. Small quantities of food or foods with low moisture content can burn, dry out or catch on fire if cooked too long. If a fire occurs, stop the oven and leave the oven door closed. Disconnect the power cord, or shut off power at the fuse or circuit breaker panel.

2. Popcorn must be popped in a microwave corn popper. Microwave corn poppers are available through many retail stores. In addition, special microwave popcorn is available in some areas of the country. This popcorn pops in its own package and does not require a microwave corn popper. It may be used in this oven.

3. Do not attempt to deep fat fry in your oven.

4. Dry only herbs and flowers in your microwave oven. Follow directions given in this cookbook and do not leave oven unattended. Drying meats, fruits, and vegetables are not recommended.

5. Do not use paper towels which contain a synthetic fiber woven into them, such as nylon. Any synthetic may cause the towel to ignite.

6. Do not use the oven for any reason other than the preparation of food. Exceptions would be specific uses indicated in this cookbook.

CANNING

DO NOT USE YOUR MICROWAVE OVEN FOR CANNING

Canning and sterilizing of canning jars should NOT be done in a microwave oven. Home canning destroys mold, yeast, bacteria, and enzymes in foods to prevent spoilage.

Low acid and nonacid foods require a temperature of 240°F which is above the boiling point of water. In canning 240°F is obtained by using a pressure canner set at 10 pounds pressure (at sea level). Your microwave oven can only bring plain water to the boiling point. (212°F).

High acid foods are processed in a hot water bath canner. The canning jars are covered by water which is kept at a rolling boil. Your microwave oven cannot duplicate this procedure. Since canning jars also need to be submerged in water for sterilization, it would be impossible to do this procedure in a microwave oven.

Improperly canned food may spoil and be dangerous to consume. We recommend that canning be done only on a conventional range top following standard canning procedures.

In addition, certain canning lids and rings may cause arcing in the microwave oven.

Appetizers

APPETIZER PÂTÉ

1 pound chicken livers, halved
½ cup chicken broth
1 medium onion, chopped
¼ teaspoon thyme
4 slices bacon, cooked and crumbled
   (see page 33)
¼ cup butter or margarine, softened
1 tablespoon sherry, optional
½ teaspoon garlic salt
Dash pepper
Parsley flakes

Yield: 1⅓ Cups

In 1½ quart bowl, combine livers, broth, onion and thyme. Cook, covered with plastic wrap, at **HIGH** 3 to 5 minutes and at **MEDIUM** 6 to 8 minutes or until livers are tender; stir once. Drain and reserve ¼ cup liquid.
In electric blender or food processor, puree liver and onion mixture, reserved liquid, bacon, butter, sherry, garlic and pepper until smooth. Spoon into crock or small bowl; sprinkle with parsley and chill. Serve as a spread with crackers.

FUN FRANKS

½ cup chili sauce
½ cup pickle relish
¼ cup beer
1 pound frankfurters, cut into 1-inch pieces

Yield: 4 Servings

In medium glass bowl, combine chili sauce, pickle relish and beer. Cover with wax paper. Cook at **HIGH** 4 minutes and at **MEDIUM** 2 to 3 minutes, or until sauce is thickened. Stir twice. Stir in frankfurters. Cook at **HIGH** 3 to 4 minutes; stir once.
Let stand, covered, 2 minutes before serving.

MEATBALL MORSELS

1 pound ground beef
1 egg
½ cup soft bread crumbs
¼ cup catsup
1 tablespoon parsley flakes
1 teaspoon onion powder
1 teaspoon salt
⅛ teaspoon pepper

Yield: 36 Meatballs

Thoroughly combine all ingredients; shape into 1-inch meatballs (about 36). Arrange 18 meatballs in 8-inch square dish. Cook at **HIGH** 4 to 6 minutes; stir once. Drain liquid. Repeat procedure with remaining meatballs.
Serve with favorite sauce or gravy.

COCKTAIL REUBENS

36 slices party-size rye bread
½ cup creamy Russian dressing
¼ pound thinly sliced corned beef
1 can (8 oz.) sauerkraut, drained
6 slices (rectangular) Swiss cheese, each
   cut into 6 pieces

Yield: 36 Hors d'oeuvres

Spread bread with dressing; top with corned beef, sauerkraut and cheese. Arrange 6 on paper plate or serving platter. Cook at **MEDIUM** 2 to 2½ minutes, or until cheese is melted. Repeat procedure with remaining ingredients.

CHEESE AND SPINACH CRUSTLESS QUICHE

4 eggs
1/3 cup half 'n half
1 1/2 cups (6 oz.) shredded Swiss cheese
1 package (10 oz.) frozen spinach, cooked and drained (see page 63)
4 slices bacon, crisp-cooked and crumbled (see page 33)
1 teaspoon lemon juice
1/2 teaspoon salt

Yield: 10 Servings

Beat eggs with half 'n half until light and fluffy in medium bowl. Blend cheese, spinach, bacon, lemon juice and salt. Pour into lightly greased 9-inch quiche dish. Cook at **MEDIUM** 11 to 13 minutes. Quiche is done when knife inserted near center comes out clean.
Let stand, uncovered, 5 minutes. Cut into 10 pieces to serve.

HOLIDAY CHEESE BALL

1 package (3 oz.) cream cheese
3 cups (12 oz.) shredded Cheddar cheese
1/4 cup flour
1/4 cup white wine
1/4 teaspoon onion powder
1/8 teaspoon garlic powder
1/8 teaspoon Worcestershire sauce
1/3 cup finely chopped nuts or parsley flakes

Yield: 1 Ball

In medium glass bowl, combine cream cheese, Cheddar cheese, flour, wine, onion, garlic and Worcestershire. Cook at **LOW** 5 to 6 minutes, or until cheese is soft. With electric mixer, beat until smooth. Shape into ball and roll in nuts; chill.
To serve, reheat at **LOW** 3 to 3 1/2 minutes or until spreadable.

CRUNCHY VEGETABLE MUNCHIES

1 head (about 1 1/2 lb.) cauliflower
1 package (2 3/8 oz.) Italian flavored seasoned coating mix

Yield: 24 Hors d'oeuvres

Cut cauliflower into about 24 flowerets; rinse. Empty coating mix into plastic bag and coat cauliflowerets. On paper plate, arrange 12 in circular pattern. Cook at **HIGH** 3 to 4 minutes, or until tender.
Let stand 2 minutes before serving; repeat procedure with remaining ingredients.

STUFFED MUSHROOM MORSELS

3/4 pound small mushrooms, cleaned
4 slices bacon, diced
1 small onion, finely chopped
1 slice bread, crumbled
2 tablespoons grated Parmesan cheese
1/4 teaspoon oregano, optional
1/8 teaspoon pepper

Yield: 32 Hors d'oeuvres

Remove stems from mushrooms; chop enough stems to equal 1/2 cup.
Place bacon and onion in 8-inch round dish. Cook at **HIGH** 3 to 4 minutes, or until bacon is crisp and onion is tender; stir occasionally. Drain.
In bowl, combine bacon, onion, chopped mushroom, bread, cheese, oregano and pepper. Stuff each mushroom cap with 1/2 tablespoon bacon mixture. In same baking dish, arrange 16 mushrooms. Cook at **HIGH** 4 1/2 to 5 minutes, or until mushrooms are tender. Repeat procedure with remaining mushrooms.

CHILI DIP OLÉ

$\frac{1}{2}$ pound ground beef
1 medium onion, finely chopped
1 envelope (1¼ oz.) chili seasoning mix
1 can (6 oz.) tomato paste
1 tablespoon sugar (optional)
Corn chips

Yield: 2 Cups

In medium glass bowl, crumble ground beef. Stir in onions. Cook at **HIGH** 3 to 4 minutes, or until beef is browned; stir once. Drain. Stir in chili seasoning, tomato paste and sugar. Cook at **HIGH** 3 to 4 minutes.
Serve warm with corn chips.

MEXICALI FIESTA DIP

1 pound pasteurized process cheese, cubed
1 can (16 oz.) whole tomatoes, drained and chopped
1 can (4 oz.) green chilies, drained and chopped
Dash hot pepper sauce
Taco chips

Yield: 3 Cups

In large glass bowl, combine cheese, tomatoes, chilies and pepper sauce. Cook at **MEDIUM** 9 to 10 minutes, or until cheese is melted; stir twice. Serve warm with taco chips.

Soups

PREPARING CONVENIENCE SOUPS

Preparing Canned Soups
- Empty contents into casserole dish or soup bowl.
- Dilute according to label directions.
- Set Power at **MEDIUM***. Heat, covered, stirring once.
- Let stand, covered, 3 minutes before serving.
- *If heating soup diluted with milk, increase heating time by 1 minute.*

SOUP	APPROX. COOKING TIME at MEDIUM (in minutes)
Condensed (10½ to 11½ oz.)	4 to 6
Semi-condensed, single serving (7½ to 7¾ oz.)	3 to 4
Ready-to-heat (19 oz.)	5 to 6
(10¾ oz.)	3 to 4

Dry Soup Mixes
- Select a casserole which is twice the volume of the water recommended on the soup mix package.
- Add water to the dish and stir.
- Set Power at **HIGH**.
- Bring to a boil.*
- Stir in soup mix.
- Set power at **MEDIUM**.
- Heat, covered, 3 to 4 minutes**; stir once.
- Stand, covered, 5 minutes, or until noodles or vegetables are tender.
  See Heating Liquids Chart, page 28 for time to bring water to a boil.
  **Heat soup mixes with broad noodles 7 to 8 minutes.*

MOM'S HOMEMADE CHICKEN SOUP

2 to 2½ pounds chicken parts
3 stalks celery, cut up
1 onion, sliced
2 bay leaves, crushed
1½ to 2 teaspoons peppercorns or pepper to taste
8 cups hot water
2 carrots, coarsely shredded (about 1 cup)
1 to 1½ cups fine egg noodles
2 teaspoons salt

Yield: 8 Servings

In 5-quart casserole, combine chicken, celery, onion, bay leaves, peppercorns and water. Cover with lid. Cook at **HIGH** 35 minutes, or until chicken is tender; stir twice. Strain broth into bowl and pour back into casserole. Add carrots, noodles and salt; cover. Cook at **HIGH** 7 to 8 minutes.

Meanwhile, remove chicken from bones. Add chicken to soup. Let stand, covered, 7 to 8 minutes, or until noodles are tender.

Want to Make Your Soup Something Special?
Just before serving, add any one, or even two, of the following:
- chopped hard-cooked egg
- chopped or sliced olives
- corn chips
- crisp, bite-size cereal
- dried chives or dill weed
- french fried onion pieces
- grated cheese
- lemon slices
- popcorn
- seasoned croutons
- sliced frankfurters
- sliced mushrooms
- slivered almonds
- small pretzel rings
- sour cream
- thin strips of cheese

CHICKEN GUMBO

1 pound chicken parts
1 medium onion, sliced
1 tablespoon flour
2 cups chicken broth
1 can (16 oz.) stewed tomatoes, chopped
1 package (10 oz.) frozen sliced okra,
  thawed (see page 63)
1 can (8 oz.) whole kernel corn
1 teaspoon salt
2 dashes hot pepper sauce
1/8 teaspoon garlic powder
Pepper to taste

Yield: 6 Servings

Arrange chicken in 3-quart casserole; cover with glass lid. Cook at **HIGH** 10 to 12 minutes, or until chicken is tender. Remove chicken and cool. Add onion to casserole. Cook at **HIGH** 4 minutes; stir in flour blended with chicken broth, tomatoes, okra, corn, salt, hot pepper sauce, garlic and pepper. Heat, covered, at **HIGH** 8 minutes and **MEDIUM** 10 to 12 minutes; stir occasionally.
Meanwhile, remove chicken from bones. Add to soup and cook, covered, at **MEDIUM** 4 to 6 minutes.
Let stand, covered, 5 minutes before serving.

SAVORY SPLIT PEA SOUP

6 cups hot water
1 package (16 oz.) dried split peas
1/2 pound bacon, diced
5 stalks celery, chopped
1 medium onion, chopped
3 carrots, sliced
1 teaspoon salt
1/8 teaspoon thyme or basil, optional
Pepper to taste

Yield: 6 Servings

Combine all ingredients in 4-quart casserole. Cover with glass lid. Heat at **HIGH** 12 minutes and at **MEDIUM** 45 to 50 minutes or until peas are tender; stir occasionally.
Put mixture through food mill or puree in food processor or blender. Reheat, adding additional water, if necessary, at **MEDIUM** 4 to 6 minutes.

MINESTRONE

Good 1/21/11

2 tablespoons butter or margarine
3 carrots, thinly sliced
1 medium onion, chopped
2 cups chicken broth
1 can (16 oz.) stewed tomatoes, chopped
1 cup shredded cabbage or zucchini
1 teaspoon basil
1 teaspoon parsley flakes
1 teaspoon salt
1 can (16 oz.) kidney beans, drained
1/4 to 1/3 cup broken spaghetti
  (about 2-inch pieces)

Yield: 4 Servings

In 3-quart casserole, combine butter, carrots and onions. Cover with glass lid. Cook at **HIGH** 5 to 7 minutes. Add broth, tomatoes, cabbage, basil, parsley and salt. Heat, covered, at **HIGH** 7 to 9 minutes; stir once. Add kidney beans and spaghetti. Heat, covered, at **MEDIUM** 13 to 15 minutes, or until spaghetti is tender; stir once. Let stand, covered, 5 minutes.

FRENCH ONION SOUP

3 tablespoons butter or margarine
3 cups sliced onions (about 3 medium)
3 cups beef broth
1 cup water
1 teaspoon Worcestershire sauce
Salt and pepper to taste
Croutons
Grated Parmesan cheese

Yield: 4 Servings

Place butter and onions in 3-quart casserole. Cover with lid. Cook at **HIGH** 8 to 9 minutes, or until onions are tender; stir twice.
Stir in broth, water, Worcestershire sauce, salt and pepper, cover. Cook at **HIGH** 12 to 13 minutes. Serve with croutons and Parmesan cheese.

GARDEN VEGETABLE SOUP

1/2 pound ground beef, browned and
  drained, optional
2 cups beef broth
1 cup hot water
1 can (16 oz.) whole tomatoes, chopped
1 medium carrot, shredded
4 stalks celery, thinly sliced
1 small onion, finely chopped
1 bay leaf
1 teaspoon salt
1/8 teaspoon pepper
Dash marjoram
Dash thyme

Yield: 4 Servings

Combine all ingredients in 2-quart casserole.
Cover with glass lid. Heat at **HIGH** 8 minutes
and at **MEDIUM** 15 to 17 minutes, or until
vegetables are tender; stir once.
Let stand, covered, 5 minutes before serving.

MANHATTAN CLAM CHOWDER

1 can (10 1/2 oz.) condensed vegetable
  soup
1 1/2 cups tomato juice or water
1 can (7 1/2 oz.) minced clams
Dash thyme

Yield: 4 Servings

Combine all ingredients in 1 1/2-quart casserole.
Cover with glass lid. Heat at **HIGH** 10 to 12
minutes; stir occasionally.
Let stand, covered, 3 minutes. Serve, if desired,
with oyster crackers.

VICHYSSOISE

3 tablespoons butter or margarine
3 medium leeks, white part, sliced
1 1/2 cups chicken broth
3/4 teaspoon salt
1/8 teaspoon pepper
2 medium potatoes, baked (see page 63)
1 1/2 cups milk
1 cup heavy cream
1 tablespoon sherry, optional
Chopped chives

Yield: 4 Servings

Combine butter and leeks in 2-quart casserole.
Cook at **HIGH** 3 to 5 minutes; stir in broth, salt
and pepper. Heat, covered with glass lid, at
HIGH 3 to 5 minutes and at **MEDIUM** 6
minutes.
Meanwhile, peel and dice potatoes. With electric
mixer, blender or food processor puree
potatoes, broth mixture and milk. Return to dish.
Reheat, covered, at **MEDIUM** 3 to 4 minutes;
stir in cream and sherry.
Chill thoroughly and garnish, if desired, with
chopped chives before serving.

CREAMY CORN CHOWDER

3 tablespoons butter or margarine
1 stalk celery finely chopped
1 teaspoon dried chives
1 teaspoon salt
1/4 teaspoon pepper
1 can (13 oz.) evaporated milk
1 can (17 oz.) cream-style corn

Yield: 4 Servings

Place butter and celery in 2-quart casserole.
Cook at **HIGH** 2 to 3 minutes, or until celery is
tender. Stir in chives, salt and pepper. Add milk
and corn; stir well. Cook at **HIGH** 6 to 7
minutes, or until hot and bubbly.
Let stand 3 minutes, before serving.

Sauces

PREPARING CONVENIENCE SAUCES

- Use a glass container twice the volume of the sauce.
- Prepare sauce ingredients according to package directions.
- A wire whisk is helpful in eliminating lumps, when stirring dry ingredients into liquids.
- If needed, melt butter at **LOW**.
- Heat sauces according to directions in chart.
- To blend flavors, when necessary, cook at **LOW**.
- Stir occasionally during heating.

ITEM	POWER	APPROX. COOKING TIME (in minutes)
Packaged Sauce and Gravy Mixes (³/₄ to 1¹/₂ oz.) prepared with water prepared with milk	**HIGH** **MEDIUM**	3 to 4 3¹/₂ to 5¹/₂
Sauces from condensed cream-style soups	**MEDIUM**	5 to 7
Spaghetti Sauce Mix (2 cup yield) prepared with tomato sauce	**HIGH→** **LOW**	3 to 4 8 to 10
prepared with tomato paste	**HIGH→** **MEDIUM**	3 to 4 5 to 10

BASIC WHITE SAUCE

2 tablespoons butter or margarine, melted
2 tablespoons flour
¹/₄ teaspoon salt, optional
1 cup milk

Yield: 1 Cup

In 1¹/₂-quart bowl, combine melted butter, flour and salt. Gradually add milk; stir until smooth. Cook at **MEDIUM** 5 to 6 minutes or until sauce is thickened. Stir occasionally.

Variations:
For CHEESE Sauce, stir in ¹/₂ to ³/₄ cup shredded cheese. Heat at MEDIUM 1 minute, if necessary, to completely melt cheese.
For CURRY Sauce, stir in 1 to 2 teaspoons curry powder.
For HORSERADISH Sauce, add 1 tablespoon prepared horseradish.
For MUSTARD Sauce, add 2 tablespoons prepared mustard and dash Worcestershire sauce.

HOMEMADE GRAVY

1 to 2 tablespoons butter or margarine
2 tablespoons flour
Salt and pepper to taste
1 cup roast drippings

Yield: 1 Cup

Place butter in 4-cup glass measure. Cook at **LOW** 1¹/₂ to 2¹/₂ minutes, or until melted. Stir in flour, salt and pepper. Gradually add drippings; stir until smooth. Cook at **HIGH** 2¹/₂ to 4 minutes, or until thickened; stir occasionally.

BARBECUE SAUCE

1 cup chili sauce
¾ cup water
¼ cup lemon juice
1 envelope (1⅜ oz.) onion soup mix
½ cup packed brown sugar
1 teaspoon dry mustard
⅛ teaspoon garlic powder

Yield: 2 Cups

Combine all ingredients in 1½-quart bowl. Cook at **HIGH** 6 minutes and at **MEDIUM** 4 to 6 minutes or until sauce is slightly thickened. Stir twice.
Use as a basting sauce on chicken, ribs, hamburgers, etc.

EASY HOLLANDAISE SAUCE

½ cup butter or margarine
¼ cup water
1 to 2 tablespoons lemon juice
Dash of cayenne pepper
3 egg yolks, slightly beaten

Yield: 1 Cup

In 1-quart glass bowl, combine butter, water, lemon juice and cayenne. Cook at **HIGH** 3 to 3½ minutes, or until butter melts and mixture boils. With wire whisk, gradually beat in egg yolks, beating constantly. Cook at **LOW** 45 to 60 seconds, or until thickened; stir twice.

BORDELAISE SAUCE

1 small onion, finely chopped
¼ cup butter or margarine
1 can (10½ oz.) condensed beef broth
4 teaspoons cornstarch
1 teaspoon parsley flakes
1 teaspoon Worcestershire sauce
1 bay leaf
⅛ teaspoon pepper
2 tablespoons sherry
2 tablespoons catsup

Yield: 1¾ Cups

Combine onion and butter in 4-cup glass measure. Cook at **HIGH** 3 to 4 minutes, or until onion is tender; stir once. Stir in beef broth, cornstarch, parsley flakes, Worcestershire and bay leaf until smooth. Cook at **HIGH** 4 to 5 minutes, or until thickened; stir twice. Stir in sherry and catsup and serve immediately.

BERNAISE SAUCE

2 tablespoons wine vinegar
1 teaspoon instant minced onion
4 egg yolks, beaten
½ cup butter or margarine
1 teaspoon tarragon

Yield: ¾ Cup

Combine vinegar and onion in small glass bowl. Cook at **HIGH** 1½ to 2 minutes. Add butter and cook at **HIGH** 2 to 2½ minutes or until melted and bubbly. Beating continually with wire whisk, slowly pour small amount of butter mixture into egg yolks, then gradually pour back into butter mixture. Stir in tarragon. Cook at **LOW** 15 to 20 seconds, until thickened; stir twice.
Serve immediately.

SWEET AND SOUR SAUCE

Water
1 can (8¼ oz.) crushed pineapple in heavy
 syrup, drained; reserve syrup
½ cup finely chopped green pepper,
 optional
¼ cup packed brown sugar
1 tablespoon soy sauce, optional
1 tablespoon cornstarch
⅓ to ½ cup cider vinegar

Yield: 2 Cups

In 2-cup glass measure, add enough water to
reserved syrup to equal ¾ cup. Stir in
pineapple, green pepper (if desired), brown
sugar and soy sauce. Cook at **HIGH** 2 to 3
minutes; stir once. Stir in cornstarch blended
with vinegar. Cook at **HIGH** 2 to 3 minutes, or
until sauce is slightly thickened; stir once.

NEWBURG SAUCE

1 cup half 'n half
1 cup milk
3 to 4 tablespoons sherry
3 tablespoons flour
3 egg yolks
Salt and pepper to taste

Yield: 2½ Cups

In medium glass bowl, combine half 'n half,
milk, sherry and flour. Cook at **MEDIUM** 6 to 8
minutes, or until sauce is slightly thickened; stir
twice. With wire whip, quickly stir in egg yolks;
season with salt and pepper. Cook at **LOW** 5 to
6 minutes, or until sauce is thickened; stir twice.

JIFFY SPAGHETTI SAUCE

1 large onion, finely chopped
2 tablespoons oil
2 cloves garlic, finely chopped
1 teaspoon oregano
⅛ teaspoon basil
2 cans (8 oz. ea.) tomato sauce
2 teaspoons sugar, optional

Yield: 2½ Cups

In medium glass bowl, combine onion, oil,
garlic, oregano and basil. Cook, covered with
plastic wrap, at **HIGH** 4 to 5 minutes, or until
onion is tender. Stir in remaining ingredients.
Cook, covered at **HIGH** 3 minutes and at
MEDIUM 3 to 4 minutes. Stir twice.

CRANBERRY SAUCE

2 cups sugar
¼ cup water
1 pound fresh cranberries
1 medium orange

Yield: 3½ Cups

Combine sugar and water in large glass bowl.
Cook at **HIGH** 4 to 5 minutes, or until sugar is
dissolved; stir once. Add cranberries and cook,
covered with plastic wrap, at **HIGH** 5 to 7
minutes, or until berries are soft.
Grate peel from orange and squeeze juice. Add
peel and juice to cranberries. Mash berries with
masher or stir well to crush; cool slightly. If
desired, add additional sugar to taste; chill
before serving.

RAISIN SAUCE FOR HAM

½ cup orange juice
½ cup water
1 tablespoon cornstarch
1 tablespoon rum, optional
½ cup raisins
⅓ cup currant jelly or apricot preserves
Dash allspice

Yield: 1½ Cups

In 1½-quart glass bowl, stir together orange
juice, water and cornstarch until blended. Stir in
rum, raisins, currant jelly and allspice.
Cook at **HIGH** 7 to 9 minutes, or until sauce is
thickened. Stir occasionally.

Beverages

MULLED WINE

3 cups Burgundy wine
8 teaspoons packed brown sugar or to taste
2 sticks cinnamon, broken
Dash nutmeg

Yield: 4 Servings

In each of 4 mugs, combine ³/₄ cup wine, 2 teaspoons sugar, ¹/₂ cinnamon stick and dash nutmeg. Heat at **HIGH** 6 to 7 minutes.

CAPE COD WARMER

3 cups cranapple or cranberry juice
8 whole allspice
8 whole cloves
4 sticks cinnamon, broken

Yield: 4 Servings

Combine all ingredients in 4-cup glass measure. Heat at **HIGH** 6 to 8 minutes and at **LOW** 8 to 9 minutes. To serve, cool slightly; strain into mugs. If desired, stir in ¹/₂ tablespoon vodka.

CAFÉ BRÛLOT

¹/₃ to ¹/₂ cup brandy
1 tablespoon sugar
3 whole cloves
1 stick cinnamon, broken
Peel of 1 lemon or orange
2 cups hot strong coffee

Yield: 6 Demitasse Servings

In 1-cup glass measure, combine brandy, sugar, cloves, cinnamon and lemon peel. Heat at **HIGH** 1¹/₂ to 2 minutes; stir. Carefully flame and strain brandy into coffee. Serve in demitasse cups and sweeten, if desired, to taste.

HOT SCOTCHIE

8 tablespoons butterscotch flavored pieces
4 cups milk
Ground cinnamon
8 tablespoons miniature marshmallows

Yield: 4 Servings

Place 2 tablespoons butterscotch in each of 4 mugs. Heat at **HIGH** 3¹/₂ to 4 minutes. For each drink, stir in 1 cup milk and dash ground cinnamon. Heat at **MEDIUM** 5 to 6 minutes; stir in marshmallows.

HEATING LIQUIDS CHART
For tea, instant coffee, hot chocolate mix, instant soups, hot cereal, recipes, etc.

DESIRED TEMPERATURE	LIQUID	AMOUNT	POWER	APPROX. COOKING TIME (in minutes)
Boiling (212°F)	Water	1 cup (8 oz.)	HIGH	3 to 4
		2 cups (16 oz.)	HIGH	5 to 6
		4 cups (32 oz.)	HIGH	9 to 10
Scalding (about 180°F)	Milk	1 cup (8 oz.)	MEDIUM	3 to 4
		2 cups (16 oz.)	MEDIUM	5¹/₂ to 6¹/₂
Steaming (for beverages about 170°F)	Water	1 mug (8 oz.)	HIGH	1¹/₂ to 2
		2 mugs (8 oz. ea.)	HIGH	3 to 4
		4 mugs (8 oz. ea.)	HIGH	6¹/₂ to 7¹/₂
		1 coffee cup (5 oz.)	HIGH	1¹/₄ to 1¹/₂
		2 coffee cups (5 oz. ea.)	HIGH	2¹/₂ to 3
		4 coffee cups (5 oz. ea.)	HIGH	6 to 7
Steaming (about 160°F)	Milk	1 mug (8 oz.)	MEDIUM	2 to 3
		2 mugs (8 oz. ea.)	MEDIUM	4¹/₂ to 5¹/₂
		4 mugs (8 oz. ea.)	MEDIUM	7 to 8
		1 coffee cup (5 oz.)	MEDIUM	1¹/₂ to 2¹/₂
		2 coffee cups (5 oz. ea.)	MEDIUM	3 to 4
		4 coffee cups (5 oz. ea.)	MEDIUM	6 to 7

WARNING: Heating liquids can erupt if not mixed with air. Do not heat liquids in your microwave oven without stirring first.

Meat

DEFROSTING MEATS

• Meat should be frozen in moisture and vapor proof wrapping materials.

• Small items such as chops, hamburger patties, etc. should be frozen in 1 or 2 piece layers.

• Remove meat from original wrapper and set on a roasting rack placed in a dish.

• Set **DEFROST** and heat for the time recommended in the chart.

• Turn meat over two or three times during defrost.

• Shield edges and unevenly shaped ends of roasts, halfway through the defrost cycle.

• Break apart ground beef, stew meat, etc. halfway through the defrost cycle. Remove any pieces that are defrosted.

• Separate chops and hamburger patties, halfway through the defrost cycle.

• Large roasts may still be icy in center. Allow to stand.

• Estimate 10 minutes per pound defrosting time for beef and 12 minutes per pound defrosting time for pork and lamb not listed on chart.

MEATS	APPROX. DEFROSTING TIME (minutes per pound) at DEFROST
Beef Roast	
Beef tenderloin	10 to 12
Chuck or rump	10 to 12
Sirloin, rolled	10 to 12
Steak	
Boneless sirloin	12 to 14
Flank	8 to 10
Miscellaneous	
Frankfurters	10 to 12
Ground beef	10 to 12
Liver	10 to 12
Pork Chops	12 to 14
Ribs	12 to 14
Roasts	12 to 14

DIRECTIONS FOR ROASTING MEATS

For best results, select roasts that are uniform in shape. Use a microwave roasting rack, or an inverted microwave safe saucer placed in a dish. Season as desired, but salt after cooking.

• Browning sauce mixed with equal parts of butter will enhance the color.

• Boneless beef and lamb roasts should be placed fat-side up on a roasting rack.

• Leg of lamb should be placed fat-side down on a roasting rack. Halfway through cooking turn roast over and shield by shank bone.

• Pork roasts should be placed fat-side down on the roasting rack. Halfway through cooking, turn roast over. Shield pork roasts by folding foil over end of rib bones and covering the thin meat by the bone.

• Halfway through cooking, shield top cut-edge of canned ham with a $1^1/_2$-inch strip of foil. Wrap strip of foil around ham and secure to body of ham with wooden toothpicks. Fold 1-inch over cut surface. If desired, glaze last 10 to 20 minutes of cooking.

• Loosely cover baking dish with wax paper to prevent spattering.

• If a large amount of juice accumulates in the bottom of the dish, drain occasionally. If desired, reserve for making gravy.

• Shield thin points of meat (less meaty portions) with aluminum foil, halfway through cooking. Wooden toothpicks can be used to hold the foil in place.

• Less tender cuts (pot roasts, etc.) should be cooked in liquid (soup, broth, etc.). Use at least $1/_2$ cup liquid per pound of meat.

• Use an oven cooking bag or covered casserole when cooking less tender cuts of meat. Select a covered casserole deep enough so that the meat does not touch the lid.

• If an oven cooking bag is used, prepare bag according to manufacturer's package directions. Do not use wire or metal twist-tie to close bag. Use nylon tie provided, otherwise use a piece of cotton string or a strip cut from the open end of the bag. Make six $1/_2$-inch slits in top of bag to allow steam to escape.

• Multiply the weight of the roast by the minimum recommended minutes per pound. Program Power and Time.

• After cooking, check internal temperature of the roast in several places, using a microwave or conventional meat thermometer. The thermometer should not touch bone or fat. If it does, the reading could be inaccurate. Generally, the lower temperatures in a roast are found in the center of the roast and in the muscle close to a large bone, such as a pork loin center rib roast. If the temperatures are lower than desired, return the roast to the oven and cook a few more minutes at the recommended power level.
DO NOT USE A CONVENTIONAL MEAT THERMOMETER IN THE MICROWAVE OVEN.

• Let stand, tented with foil, 10 to 15 minutes. Stand time allows the internal temperature to equalize throughout the food and thereby finishes the cooking process. During stand time the internal temperature rises 5°F to 15°F.

MEAT ROASTING CHART

MEAT	POWER	APPROX. COOKING TIME (minutes per pound)	APPROXIMATE TEMPERATURE AFTER STANDING**
Beef Roasts (up to 4 lb.)			
Rare	MEDIUM	6 to 9	125° to 135°F
Medium	MEDIUM	9 to 13½	135° to 145°F
Well	MEDIUM	12 to 16	170° to 175°F
*Pot Roast (Chuck, Rump, Flank, Brisket)	LOW	25 to 30	—
Pork			
Roast			
Bone-In	MEDIUM	12 to 13	170° to 175°F
Boneless	MEDIUM	10½ to 12	170° to 175°F
Ham (fully cooked)			
Canned (3 lb.)	MEDIUM	7½ to 9	120° to 130°F
Shank (up to 7 lb.)	MEDIUM	9½ to 10	120° to 130°F
Chops ½" thick	MEDIUM	8½ to 10	—
Lamb			
Roast			
Bone-In			
Medium	MEDIUM	9 to 11	150° to 160°F
Well	MEDIUM	12 to 14½	170° to 175°F
Boneless			
Medium	MEDIUM	9½ to 11	150° to 160°F
Well	MEDIUM	12 to 13	170° to 175°F
Chops ½" thick	MEDIUM	6 to 7	—

*These meats should be cooked in an oven cooking bag or covered casserole surrounded with liquid.
**Check meat with a conventional meat thermometer. If the meat is not cooked to the desired temperature, return it to the oven and cook a few more minutes at the recommended power level.

PREPARING CONVENIENCE MEATS

- Arrange meats in shallow baking dish. Cover loosely with wax paper to prevent spatter.
- To cook bacon, line bottom of 8-inch square dish or glass pie plate with a paper towel.
- Place bacon in dish; cover loosely with another paper towel to prevent spatter.
- A maximum of 4 slices of bacon can be cooked at one time in oven.

ITEM	AMOUNT	POWER	APPROX. COOKING TIME (in minutes)	STAND TIME (in minutes)
Beef Patties, frozen (3½ oz. ea.)	1 2 4	MEDIUM	3½ to 4½ 5½ to 6½ 9 to 9½	2 3 3
Bacon, slices	2 3 4	HIGH	2½ to 3 3½ to 4 4½ to 5	1 1 1
Canadian bacon slices (2 oz.)	2 4	HIGH	2 to 3 3 to 4	3 3
Frankfurters, scored	2 4	HIGH	2½ to 3½ 4 to 4½	3 3
Ham, slices (about 2 oz. ea.)	2	HIGH	3 to 4	3
Hamburgers (4 oz. ea.)	1 2 4	HIGH	1½ to 2 2½ to 3 3½ to 4	2 2 2
Sausage Links, frozen, (precooked, brown and serve)	2 4	HIGH	2 to 3 3 to 4	2 2
†Sausage Links, fresh (1 to 2 oz. ea.)	2 4	HIGH	3 to 4 5 to 6	3 3
Sausage Patties fresh (1 to 2 oz. ea.)	2 4	HIGH	2 to 4 4 to 5	2 2

†*Special Hint: Pierce with fork and brush with browning sauce before cooking.*

Beef

BEEF WITH BROCCOLI

1 tablespoon oil
¾ pound boneless steak, cut into thin
  strips
1 clove garlic, finely chopped
⅛ teaspoon ground ginger
1½ cups broccoli flowerets
1 tablespoon cornstarch
½ cup beef broth
1 tablespoon sherry
1 tablespoon soy sauce
Toasted sesame seeds

Yield: 2—3 Servings

Place oil in 8-inch square dish. Cook at **HIGH** 2
minutes. Stir in beef, garlic and ginger. Cook at
HIGH 4 to 5 minutes. Stir twice. Add broccoli.
Cover with plastic wrap. Cook at **HIGH** 4 to 6
minutes or until broccoli is crisp tender. Stir
once. Stir in cornstarch blended with broth,
sherry, and soy sauce. Cook at **HIGH** 4 to 5
minutes, or until sauce is thickened. Stir once.
Top with sesame seeds.

BEEF BOURGUIGNON

¼ cup butter or margarine
1½ pounds boneless beef, cut into 1-inch
  cubes
3 tablespoons brandy
1 cup beef broth, divided
½ cup Burgundy wine
2 bay leaves
⅛ teaspoon pepper
1 jar (16 oz.) whole boiled onions, drained
  and rinsed
¼ pound fresh mushrooms, halved or 1 jar
  (4½ oz.) sliced mushrooms, drained
¼ cup flour

Yield: 6 Servings

Place butter in 4-quart casserole. Cook at **HIGH**
1 to 2 minutes, or until melted. Add beef. Cook
at **HIGH** 4 to 6 minutes; stir once.
In small glass bowl, heat brandy at **HIGH** ½ to
1 minute; carefully flame. Stir into beef with
½ cup broth, wine, bay leaves and pepper.
Cover with glass lid. Cook at **HIGH** 5 minutes
and at **LOW** 30 to 40 minutes, or until beef is
almost tender; stir occasionally.
Add onions and mushrooms. Blend flour and
remaining broth until smooth. Stir into beef
mixture. Cook, covered, at **HIGH** 4 to 5
minutes; stir once.

BEEF IN SOUR CREAM SAUCE

2 tablespoons butter or margarine
1 pound boneless round beef steak, cut
  into thin strips
1 large onion, finely chopped
Salt and pepper to taste
1 package (¾ oz.) mushroom gravy mix
1 cup water
1 jar (4½ oz.) sliced mushrooms, drained
½ cup sour cream

Yield: 4 Servings

Place butter in 8-inch round dish. Cook at **HIGH**
1 to 2 minutes. Stir in steak, onion, salt and
pepper. Cook at **HIGH** 8 to 9 minutes; stir
occasionally.
Let stand, covered, 5 minutes.
Meanwhile, in glass bowl, combine gravy mix,
water and mushrooms. Cook at **HIGH** 5 to 6
minutes, or until thickened; stir twice. Stir in
sour cream until smooth. Blend gravy with
steak. If necessary, reheat at **LOW** 2 to 3
minutes before serving.

BEST BEEF GOULASH

2 pounds boneless beef, cut into 1-inch
  cubes
2¼ cups, water, divided
1 envelope (1⅜ oz.) onion soup mix
1 can (3 oz.) whole mushrooms, drained
2 tablespoons paprika
¼ teaspoon caraway seeds
3 tablespoons cornstarch

Yield: 6—8 Servings

In 4-quart casserole, combine beef, 2 cups
water, onion soup mix, mushrooms, paprika and
caraway seeds. Cook, covered with a glass lid,
at **HIGH** 10 minutes and at **LOW** 55 to 60
minutes, or until beef is tender. Stir
occasionally.
Blend cornstarch with remaining ¼ cup water,
until smooth. Stir into beef mixture. Cook,
uncovered, at **LOW** 3 minutes, or until
thickened.

FLANK STEAK FLORENTINE

1/4 pound fresh mushrooms
1 large onion, finely chopped
1 clove garlic, finely chopped
3 tablespoons butter or margarine
1 package (10 oz.) frozen chopped spinach, defrosted and drained (see page 100)
1 beef flank steak (1 1/2 to 1 3/4 lb.)
2 beef bouillon cubes
1 cup hot water
1 can (10 3/4 oz.) condensed golden mushroom soup
2 tablespoons dry vermouth, optional

Yield: 4 Servings

Chop 1/2 cup mushrooms. Combine with onion, garlic and butter. Cook at **HIGH** 5 to 6 minutes, or until onion and mushrooms are tender. Stir in spinach. Pound flank steak with a mallet; spread spinach mixture down center of steak. Roll steak lengthwise around filling; tie with cotton string or secure with wooden toothpicks. Place seam side down in 8-inch dish. Slice remaining mushrooms and combine with bouillon, water, soup and vermouth. Cover with plastic wrap. Cook at **HIGH** 10 minutes and at **LOW** 25 to 30 minutes, or until steak is tender.
Let stand, covered, 10 minutes, before serving.

SWISS STEAK SPECIAL

1 pound boneless round steak, cut into individual servings and pounded 1/4-inch thin.
1 can (16 oz.) whole tomatoes, chopped
1 can (8 oz.) tomato sauce
1 envelope (1 3/8 oz.) onion or onion-mushroom soup mix
1 teaspoon basil
1/4 teaspoon garlic powder
4 slices (4 oz.) mozzarella cheese

Yield: 4 Servings

Arrange steak in 8-inch square dish. Combine tomatoes, sauce, soup mix, basil and garlic. Pour over steak. Cover with plastic wrap. Cook at **HIGH** 6 to 7 minutes and at **LOW** 45 to 50 minutes. Top with cheese.
Let stand, covered, 5 minutes.

TERIYAKI BEEF KABOBS

2 tablespoons packed brown sugar
2 tablespoons soy sauce
1 tablespoon lemon juice
1 tablespoon oil
1 pound boneless steak, cut into 1 1/2-inch cubes
1/2 pint cherry tomatoes
1 medium green pepper, cut into chunks

Yield: 4 Servings.

In glass bowl, combine sugar, soy sauce, lemon juice and oil; add steak. If desired, cover and marinate in refrigerator at least 3 hours; stir occasionally.
On four 9 or 10-inch wooden skewers, alternately thread steak, tomatoes and green pepper. Arrange skewers on 8-inch square dish. Cook at **MEDIUM** 10 to 12 minutes, or until meat is medium-rare. Turn skewers over halfway through cooking.

PEPPER STEAK

2 tablespoons oil
1 pound boneless beef steak, cut into thin strips
2 tablespoons soy sauce
Dash ginger
2 medium green peppers, cut into chunks
2 medium onions, sliced
1 tablespoon cornstarch
1/2 cup beef broth

Yield: 4 Servings

Place oil in 8-inch square dish. Cook at **HIGH** 2 minutes. Stir in meat, soy sauce and ginger. Cook at **HIGH** 3 to 4 minutes; stir once. Push meat to center of dish. Place green peppers and onions around sides of dish. Cover with wax paper. Cook at **HIGH** 4 minutes.
Meanwhile, blend cornstarch with broth; stir until smooth. Heat at **HIGH** 2 to 3 minutes, or until thickened; stir once. Stir into meat mixture. Cook, uncovered, at **HIGH** 1 to 2 minutes to heat. If desired, serve over rice.

CORNED BEEF DINNER

4 medium potatoes
2 pounds corned beef brisket
2 onions, quartered
1½ cups water
¾ pound cabbage, cut into 4 wedges

Yield: 4 Servings

Cook potatoes 15 minutes (see page 63).
Cool, then peel.
In 2-quart casserole, place corned beef,
onions, and water. Cook, covered with glass
lid, at **HIGH** 10 minutes and **LOW** 90 minutes,
or until beef is tender. Remove to serving
platter; let stand, covered, 15 minutes.
Meanwhile remove all but ½ cup cooking liquid
from casserole. Arrange potatoes and cabbage,
thick sides toward edge of dish. Cook, covered
with glass lid, at **HIGH** 12 to 16 minutes, or
until tender.
Slice corned beef and serve with vegetables.

GOURMET POT ROAST

3 pound boneless bottom round beef roast
1½ cups dry red wine
1 can (10½ oz.) beef broth
1 medium onion, sliced
½ teaspoon thyme leaves
¼ to ½ teaspoon salt
¼ teaspoon basil
⅛ teaspoon pepper
1 regular size (10″ × 16″) oven cooking bag

Yield: 6 Servings

Prepare cooking bag according to package
directions and place in 2-quart casserole. Add
beef, wine, beef broth, onion, thyme, salt,
basil and pepper in bag. Pull bag up around
beef. Close with nylon tie or cotton string;
make six half-inch slits in top of bag.
Cook at **HIGH** 8 minutes and **LOW** 1¼ to 1½
hours, or until beef is tender.
Let stand, covered, 10 minutes. Skim off excess
fat from liquid. If desired, thicken wine mixture
for gravy.

RANCHERO POT ROAST

1 teaspoon garlic salt
½ to 1 teaspoon pepper
¼ teaspoon paprika
3 to 3¼ pound bottom round beef roast
1 cup beef broth
½ cup chili sauce
2 tablespoons onion flakes
1 regular size (10″ × 16″) oven cooking bag

Yield: 8 Servings

Prepare cooking bag according to package
directions. Combine garlic, pepper and
paprika; rub over roast. Place in cooking bag
and add broth, chili sauce and onion. Set bag
in 2-quart casserole; pull bag up around roast.
Close with nylon tie or cotton string; make six
half-inch slits in top of bag. Cook at **HIGH** 8
minutes and at **LOW** 1¼ to 1½ hours, or until
beef is tender.
Let stand 10 minutes.

CHILI BEEF LIVER

4 slices bacon
1 pound beef liver, thinly sliced
2 tablespoons flour
1 can (10½ oz.) condensed onion soup
1 can (4 oz.) sliced mushrooms, drained
¼ cup chili sauce or catsup

Yield: 4 Servings

Arrange bacon in 8-inch square dish. Cook,
covered with paper towel, at **HIGH** 5 to 6
minutes. Discard paper towel. Remove bacon,
crumble and reserve.
Coat liver lightly with flour; arrange in same
dish. Cook at **HIGH** 2 minutes. Turn liver over;
add soup, mushrooms and chili sauce. Cook,
covered with plastic wrap, at **HIGH** 5 minutes,
and at **MEDIUM** 10 to 12 minutes or until liver
is tender. Stir once.
Top with reserved bacon. Serve, if desired, over
rice.

APPLE CIDER STEW

1½ pounds boneless beef, cut into 1-inch cubes
½ small turnip, diced
½ pound green beans, cut into 1½-inch pieces
1½ cups apple cider
1 large onion, sliced
2 tablespoons catsup
1½ teaspoons salt
1 bay leaf
⅛ teaspoon pepper
⅛ teaspoon thyme
2 tablespoons flour
¼ cup water

Yield: 6 Servings

In 4-quart casserole, combine beef, turnips, green beans, cider, onion, catsup, salt, bay leaf, pepper and thyme. Cover with glass lid. Cook at **HIGH** 8 minutes and at **LOW** 1 to 1¼ hours, or until beef is tender. Stir occasionally.
Blend flour with water, until smooth. Stir into stew. Cook at **HIGH** 4 to 5 minutes, or until stew is thickened; stir twice.

BEEF STEW

2 pounds boneless beef, cut into 1-inch cubes
2 cups water, divided
1 envelope (1⅜ oz.) onion soup mix
4 medium carrots, thinly sliced
2 potatoes, peeled and cut into 1-inch cubes
1 bay leaf
1 can (8 oz.) green peas, drained
¼ cup flour

Yield: 6—8 Servings

In 4-quart casserole, combine beef, 1½ cups water, soup mix, carrots, potatoes and bay leaf. Cover with glass lid. Cook at **HIGH** 8 minutes, and at **LOW** 1 to 1¼ hours, or until beef and vegetables are tender. Stir occasionally.
Stir in peas. Blend flour and remaining water, until smooth. Stir into stew. Cook at **HIGH** 4 to 5 minutes, or until stew is thickened; stir once.

TERRIFIC BEER STEW

1½ pounds boneless beef, cut into 1-inch cubes
1 cup beef broth
½ cup beer
1 tablespoon packed brown sugar
1½ teaspoons salt
½ teaspoon pepper
½ teaspoon caraway seeds
1 large onion, sliced
1 package (10 oz.) frozen green peas, broken into pieces
3 tablespoons flour
¼ cup water
½ teaspoon browning sauce, optional
1 regular size (10″ × 16″) oven cooking bag

Yield: 6 Servings

Prepare cooking bag according to package directions. Place cooking bag in 2-quart casserole. Combine beef, broth, beer, sugar, salt, pepper and caraway in bag, turning bag several times to mix. Pull bag up around beef and close with nylon tie or cotton string; make six half-inch slits in top of bag. Cook at **HIGH** 8 minutes and at **LOW** 20 to 25 minutes. Add onions and peas; reclose. Cook at **LOW** 30 minutes, or until beef and vegetables are tender. Carefully open bag and turn down sides. Blend flour with water and browning sauce, until smooth. Stir into stew. Cook at **HIGH** 2 to 2½ minutes, or until slightly thickened.

BARBECUED BEEF SANDWICHES

½ to ¾ pound thin sliced cooked roast beef, cut into ½-inch strips
¾ cup barbecue sauce
8 slices rye bread or 4 hamburger rolls, toasted

Yield: 4 Sandwiches

Combine beef and barbecue sauce in 2-quart casserole. Cook at **HIGH** 4 to 5 minutes or until hot. Spoon onto rye bread.

Ground Beef

MEAT LOAF

1 pound ground beef
1 egg
1/3 cup dry bread crumbs
1/3 cup catsup
2 tablespoons milk
1/4 teaspoon onion powder
Salt and pepper to taste

Yield: 4 Servings

Thoroughly combine all ingredients. Shape into a loaf and place in 8-inch square dish. Cover with wax paper. Cook at **MEDIUM** 14 to 16 minutes.
Let stand, covered, 3 minutes.

SAVORY STUFFED GREEN PEPPERS

1/2 pound ground beef
1 small onion, finely chopped
1 can (8 oz.) tomato sauce, divided
2 tablespoons water
1 1/2 tablespoons grated Parmesan cheese
1/2 teaspoon salt
Pinch pepper
1/4 cup instant rice
2 medium green peppers

Yield: 2—4 Servings

Crumble ground beef into 1 1/2-quart glass bowl. Stir in onion. Cook at **HIGH** 2 to 4 minutes or until beef is brown; stir once. Drain.
Stir in 1/2 cup tomato sauce, water, 1 tablespoon cheese, salt and pepper. Cover with plastic wrap. Cook at **HIGH** 2 to 4 minutes. Stir in rice. Let stand, covered, 5 minutes.
Meanwhile, cut peppers in half lengthwise; remove seeds, rinse. Mound beef-rice filling into each half; place in 8-inch square dish. Top with remaining sauce and cheese. Cover with plastic wrap. Cook at **HIGH** 6 to 8 minutes, or until peppers are tender.
Let stand, covered, 5 minutes.

SALISBURY STEAK

1 can (4 oz.) sliced mushrooms, drained, divided
1 pound ground beef
1 can (10 3/4 oz.) condensed golden mushroom soup, divided
1 egg
1/2 cup milk, divided
1/3 cup dry bread crumbs
1 small onion, finely chopped
1/8 teaspoon pepper

Yield: 6 Servings

Chop half of mushrooms. In large bowl, combine chopped mushrooms, ground beef, 1/4 cup of soup, egg, 2 tablespoons milk, bread crumbs, onion and pepper. Shape into 4 patties. Arrange in 8-inch square dish. Cover with wax paper. Cook at **HIGH** 9 to 10 minutes. Drain. Let stand, covered, 5 minutes.
Meanwhile, in small glass bowl, combine remaining soup, mushrooms and milk. Heat at **HIGH** 2 to 3 minutes. Stir once. Pour sauce over patties and garnish, if desired, with parsley.

SWEDISH MEATBALLS

1 pound ground beef
1 egg
1/2 cup dry bread crumbs
1/2 cup milk, divided
1 small onion, finely chopped
1 tablespoon finely chopped parsley
1/2 teaspoon salt
1/8 teaspoon allspice
1/8 teaspoon pepper
1 can (10 3/4 oz.) condensed golden mushroom soup

Good — 11-23-08

used 1/2 can of chicken w/ mush.

Yield: 4 Servings

Combine ground beef, egg, bread crumbs, 1/4 cup milk, onion, parsley, salt, allspice and pepper. Shape into 1 1/4-inch meatballs (about 20). Arrange in 8-inch square dish. Cover with wax paper. Cook at **HIGH** 6 to 8 minutes; stir once. In small bowl, blend soup and remaining milk. Pour over meatballs. Cook, covered, at **MEDIUM** 4 to 5 minutes, or until heated through.
Serve, if desired, over buttered noodles, sprinkled with additional parsley.

HAMBURGER MEDLEY

1 pound ground beef
1 green pepper, chopped
1 can (15 oz.) tomato sauce
1 cup hot water
1 can (8 oz.) whole kernel corn, drained
1 cup uncooked elbow macaroni
1/8 teaspoon hot pepper sauce
Salt and pepper to taste
1 cup corn chips, crushed

Yield: 4 Servings

Crumble ground beef in 3-quart casserole. Stir in green pepper. Cook at **HIGH** 5 to 6 minutes or until beef is browned; stir once. Drain.
Stir in tomato sauce, water, corn, macaroni, hot pepper sauce, salt and pepper. Cover with glass lid. Cook at **HIGH** 10 minutes and at **MEDIUM** 8 to 9 minutes, or until macaroni is tender; stir twice.
Let stand, covered, 10 minutes. Top with corn chips, before serving.

TEXAS CHILI

1 pound ground beef
1 large onion, chopped
1/4 teaspoon garlic powder
1 can (16 oz.) kidney beans, drained
1 can (16 oz.) stewed tomatoes, broken
1 can (8 oz.) tomato sauce
2 to 3 tablespoons chili powder

Yield: 4 Servings

Crumble ground beef in 3-quart casserole. Stir in remaining ingredients. Cover with glass lid.
Cook at **HIGH** 8 minutes and at **MEDIUM** 25 to 30 minutes; stir occasionally.

MEAT LOAF MELTWICH

Chili sauce
4 slices rye bread
4 thin slices cooked meat loaf
2 slices (rectangular) Muenster cheese, halved

Yield: 2 Servings

Spread chili sauce on bread. On two slices, place meat loaf and cheese; top with remaining bread. Wrap each sandwich in paper napkin; arrange on oven tray. Cook at **MEDIUM** 2 to 2 1/2 minutes, or until heated through.

SLOPPY JOES

1 pound ground beef
1 small onion, finely chopped
1/2 to 3/4 cup catsup
1/4 cup sweet pickle relish
Salt and pepper to taste
4 hamburger rolls

Yield: 4 Sandwiches

Crumble ground beef into 8-inch square dish. Stir in onion. Cook at **HIGH** 3 to 4 minutes, or until beef is browned; stir once. Drain. Stir in catsup, relish, salt and pepper. Cover with plastic wrap. Cook at **HIGH** 7 to 8 minutes; stir twice. Serve on hamburger rolls.

ARMENIAN LUNCH

1 1/2 pounds ground beef
1 envelope (1 oz.) onion-mushroom soup mix, divided
2 cloves garlic, finely chopped
1 can (8 oz.) stewed tomatoes, chopped and drained
1 tablespoon chopped fresh parsley
1 cup (8 oz.) plain yogurt
1/2 cup chopped green pepper
Pinch dried mint leaves
4 individual loaves Middle Eastern pocket (pita) bread

Yield: 4 Servings

Crumble ground beef in 2-quart casserole. Stir in 3 tablespoons soup mix and garlic. Cover with glass lid. Cook at **HIGH** 6 to 7 minutes, or until beef is browned; stir once. Drain.
Stir in tomatoes and parsley. Cook, covered, at **HIGH** 1 minute and at **MEDIUM** 4 to 5 minutes; stir once.
Let stand, covered, 3 minutes.
Meanwhile, combine remaining soup mix, yogurt, green pepper and mint. Cut bread in half. Gently open each half and fill "pocket" with beef mixture; top with yogurt dressing.

Veal

VEAL CUTLETS WITH CAPER SAUCE

1 egg
1/4 cup water
2 veal cutlets (1/2 lb.), pounded thin
1/4 cup seasoned dry bread crumbs
1/4 teaspoon paprika
1 tablespoon oil
1 1/2 teaspoons butter or margarine
1 1/2 teaspoons flour
1/4 cup milk
1/4 cup sour cream
1 tablespoon capers

Yield: 2 Servings

Beat egg with water. Dip cutlets in egg mixture, then in bread crumbs mixed with paprika. Coat bottom of 8-inch square dish with oil; place cutlets in dish. Cook at **HIGH** 3 to 4 minutes. Halfway through cooking, turn cutlets over; drain on paper towel. Remove to serving platter and let stand, covered, 5 minutes.
Meanwhile, in small glass bowl, cook butter at **MEDIUM** 1 minute, or until melted; stir in flour, then milk. Cook at **HIGH** 1 1/2 to 2 minutes, or until thickened; stir once. Stir in sour cream and capers; if necessary, reheat at **LOW** 1/2 to 1 minute. Serve over cutlets.

WURST MIT KRAUT

6 tablespoons butter or margarine
2 medium onions, chopped
2 medium apples, sliced
2 cans (16 oz. ea.) sauerkraut, drained and rinsed
1/2 cup beef broth
1/4 teaspoon caraway seeds
1/4 teaspoon pepper
6 knockwurst sausages (3 oz. ea.)

Yield: 6 Servings

Combine butter and onion in 3-quart casserole. Cook at **HIGH** 3 to 4 minutes; stir in apples. Cook at **HIGH** 4 to 5 minutes. Stir in sauerkraut, broth, caraway and pepper. Score knockwurst diagonally and arrange on sauerkraut mixture. Cook at **HIGH** 9 to 12 minutes; rearrange knockwurst once.
Let stand, covered, 5 minutes. Garnish, if desired, with additional apple slices and parsley.

VEAL CUTLETS CORDON BLEU

4 veal cutlets or chicken cutlets (1 lb.) pounded thin
2 thin slices cooked ham, halved
2 slices (rectangular) Swiss cheese, halved
1 cup seasoned dry bread crumbs
1/2 teaspoon salt
1/8 teaspoon pepper
Dash allspice
1 egg, beaten with 1/4 cup water
3 tablespoons oil

Yield: 4 Servings

On one side of each cutlet, place ham and cheese; fold cutlet in half. Pound edges together to seal or secure with wooden toothpicks. Dip cutlets in bread crumbs mixed with salt, pepper and allspice; dip in egg, then again in bread crumbs. Coat bottom of 8-inch square dish with half of oil; place cutlets in dish. Sprinkle remaining oil on cutlets. Cook at **HIGH** 7 to 8 minutes; halfway through cooking, turn cutlets over.
Let stand, covered with wax paper, 5 minutes.

VEAL PAPRIKA

1 pound boneless veal, cut into 1 1/2-inch cubes
1/2 pound fresh mushrooms, sliced
1 cup chicken broth, divided
1 medium onion, finely chopped
1/2 to 1 teaspoon paprika
1/2 to 1 teaspoon salt
1/8 to 1/4 teaspoon pepper
Dash caraway seeds
2 to 3 tablespoons flour
1/2 cup sour cream

Yield: 4 Servings

In 2-quart casserole, combine veal, mushrooms, 1/2 cup broth, onion, paprika, salt, pepper and caraway. Cover with glass lid. Cook at **HIGH** 10 minutes and at **MEDIUM** 13 to 15 minutes, or until veal is tender; stir occasionally.
Blend flour with remaining 1/2 cup broth; stir until smooth. Stir into dish. Cook at **HIGH** 2 to 3 minutes, or until sauce is thickened. Blend in sour cream.

Pork

STUFFED PORK CHOPS

1 tablespoon butter or margarine
1 stalk celery, thinly sliced
1 small onion, finely chopped
¾ cup seasoned croutons
5 tablespoons beef broth or water, divided
2 rib-cut pork chops, ¾-inch thick (1¼ lb.)
Pepper
Browning Sauce

Yield: 2 Servings

Melt butter in 8-inch square dish at **HIGH** 30 seconds. Add celery and onion. Cook at **HIGH** 3 to 4 minutes, or until celery and onion are tender; stir twice. In bowl, combine celery, onion, croutons and 3 tablespoons broth; stir until broth is absorbed.
Cut pocket in each chop for stuffing; season with pepper. Stuff chops with crouton mixture; secure with wooden toothpicks.
In the same dish, arrange chops rib end toward center; add remaining broth. Brush chops with browning sauce mixed with a little water. Cook, covered with plastic wrap, at **MEDIUM** 11 to 12 minutes, or until chops are tender. Halfway through cooking, turn chops over; cover.
Let stand, covered, 5 minutes.

LEMON BAKED PORK CHOPS

4 pork chops, ½-inch thick
1 medium onion, thinly sliced
¼ cup chili sauce
1 tablespoon water
2 teaspoons brown gravy mix
½ teaspoon salt
⅛ teaspoon pepper
4 lemon slices

Yield: 4 Servings

Arrange pork chops in 8-inch square dish. Top with onion slices. In small bowl, combine chili sauce, water, gravy mix, salt and pepper; pour over pork chops. Top with lemon slice. Cover with wax paper. Cook at **MEDIUM** 14 minutes, or until pork chops are done.
Let stand, covered, 5 minutes before serving.

OVEN-FRIED PORK CHOPS

2 rib-cut pork chops, ½-inch thick
1 package (2⅜ oz.) seasoned coating mix for pork

Coat chops with coating mix according to package directions. Arrange chops rib end toward center in paper towel lined 8-inch square dish. Cover with wax paper. Cook at **MEDIUM** 5½ to 7 minutes. Halfway through cooking, turn chops over.
Let stand, covered, 5 minutes before serving.

PEACHY PORK ROAST

Water
1 can (8½ oz.) sliced peaches, drained and chopped; reserve syrup
1 package (6 oz.) stuffing mix for pork with seasoning packet
1 egg
⅓ cup chopped walnuts
¼ cup butter or margarine
3 to 3¼ pound pork rib roast
¼ cup peach preserves

Yield: 6 Servings

Add enough water to reserved syrup to equal 1½ to 1¾ cups in 2-cup glass measure. Cook at **HIGH** 3 to 3½ minutes or until hot. In medium glass bowl, combine liquid with peaches, stuffing mix (and included seasoning packet), egg, walnuts and butter; stir until liquid is absorbed and butter is melted.
Cut pockets in pork roast, one opposite each bone. Stuff each pocket with 2 tablespoons stuffing; secure with cotton string or wooden toothpicks. In 8-inch square dish, arrange roast fat-side-down on microwave roasting rack. Cover with wax paper.
Cook at **MEDIUM** 12 to 13 minutes per pound. Halfway through cooking, turn over; brush on peach preserves.
Let stand, covered, 10 minutes before serving. Meanwhile, reheat remaining stuffing at **MEDIUM** 6 to 7 minutes; stir twice.
Serve with roast. To carve roast, remove string; cut in between each bone.

SWEET AND SOUR PORK

1 can (8¼ oz.) chunk pineapple in heavy
   syrup, drained; reserve ⅓ cup syrup
¼ cup white vinegar
1 tablespoon cornstarch
2 tablespoons oil
1 pound boneless pork, cut into ¾-inch
   cubes
¼ cup soy sauce
1 bunch green onions, thinly sliced
1 green pepper, cut into small chunks

Yield: 4 Servings

In small glass bowl, combine reserved syrup,
vinegar and cornstarch. Cook at **HIGH** 2 to 2½
minutes, or until thickened; stir once.
Place oil in 8-inch square dish. Cook at **HIGH** 2
minutes; stir in pork, soy sauce and onions.
Cook at **HIGH** 7 to 8 minutes; stir twice. Add
green pepper and pineapple; cook covered with
plastic wrap, at **HIGH** 3 to 4 minutes, or until
pork is tender.
Stir in sauce and let stand, covered, 5 minutes.

CHINESE PORK AND GREEN VEGETABLES

1 pound boneless pork, cut into thin strips
2 tablespoons soy sauce
⅛ teaspoon garlic powder
1 package (6 oz.) frozen pea pods,
   defrosted (see page 100)
2 bunches green onions, cut into ¾-inch
   pieces
1½ to 2 tablespoons cornstarch
1 cup beef broth

Yield: 4 Servings

In 8-inch square dish, combine pork, soy sauce
and garlic. Cook at **HIGH** 6 to 7 minutes; stir
occasionally. Add pea pods and green onions.
Cook, covered with plastic wrap, at **HIGH** 3 to
4 minutes, or until pork is tender; stir once.
Blend cornstarch with broth until smooth. Stir
into pork mixture. Cook at **HIGH** 4 to 5
minutes, or until sauce is slightly thickened; stir
occasionally. Serve, if desired, over rice.

SOUTHERN BARBECUED RIBS

1 cup barbecue sauce
2 tablespoons flour
2 tablespoons honey or dark corn syrup
1 tablespoon soy sauce
2 pound pork spareribs, cut into individual
   ribs
1 regular size (10″ × 16″) oven cooking bag

Yield: 4 Servings

Prepare cooking bag according to package
directions. In cooking bag, combine barbecue
sauce, flour, honey and soy sauce; add ribs and
turn bag to coat. Set cooking bag in 2-quart
casserole. Pull bag up around ribs with nylon tie
or cotton string; make six half-inch slits in top
of bag.
Cook at **HIGH** 10 minutes and at **LOW** 25 to 30
minutes, or until ribs are tender. Halfway
through cooking rearrange ribs.

CRANBERRY GLAZED HAM

¾ cup cranberry juice
¼ cup orange juice
¼ cup packed brown sugar
¼ cup raisins
1 tablespoon cornstarch
Dash cloves
3 pound canned ham
Whole cloves

Yield: 10—12 Servings

In small glass bowl combine juices, sugar,
raisins, cornstarch and cloves. Stir until smooth.
Cook at **HIGH** 3 to 4 minutes, or until glaze is
thickened; stir once. Decorate ham with whole
cloves. Shield top cut-edge with 1½-inch wide
strip of foil.
Wrap foil around ham and secure to the body of
the ham with wooden toothpicks. Place ham in
microwave roasting rack in 8-inch square dish.
Cover with wax paper. Cook at **HIGH** 24 to 30
minutes. Halfway through cooking, turn ham
over and spoon on half of the glaze; baste
occasionally with remaining glaze.
Let stand, covered, 10 minutes before serving.

SPICY SAUSAGE STEW

1 pound Italian sausage links, cut into
   1½-inch pieces
1 pound boneless pork, cut into 1-inch
   cubes
1 can (8 oz.) whole tomatoes, chopped
1 can (8 oz.) tomato sauce
1 green pepper, cut into chunks
1 teaspoon basil
1 teaspoon oregano
½ teaspoon garlic powder

Yield: 6 Servings

Place sausage in 3-quart casserole. Cook at
HIGH 6 to 8 minutes; stir once. Drain. Add
remaining ingredients. Cook, covered with glass
lid, at **HIGH** 10 minutes and at **LOW** 1 hour, or
until pork is tender; stir occasionally. Serve, if
desired, with rice or pasta.

SAUSAGE AND BEAN CASSOULET

1 pound Italian sausage links, cut into
   1½-inch pieces
1 small onion, sliced
2 cans (16 oz. ea.) navy or small white
   beans, rinsed
½ pound cooked ham, cut into 1-inch
   pieces
1 can (8 oz.) tomato sauce
½ cup catsup
¼ cup white wine, optional
¼ cup packed brown sugar
1 teaspoon salt
½ teaspoon dry mustard
¼ teaspoon pepper

Yield: 4—6 Servings

Combine sausage and onions in 3-quart
casserole. Cook, covered with glass lid, at **HIGH**
10 to 12 minutes, or until sausage is almost
cooked; stir once. Drain. Stir in remaining
ingredients. Cook, covered, at **HIGH** 8 minutes,
and at **MEDIUM** 15 to 17 minutes, or until
flavors are blended; stir twice.
Let stand, covered, 5 minutes.

GLAZED HAM STEAK

⅓ cup apricot preserves
¼ cup raisins
Dash allspice, cinnamon or cloves
1 pound fully cooked ham steak, ¾-inch
   thick

Yield: 4 Servings

In small glass bowl, combine preserves, raisins
and allspice. Cook at **HIGH** 1 to 2 minutes, or
until preserves are melted. Place ham in 9-inch
pie plate. Cook at **MEDIUM** 7 to 9 minutes.
Drain excess liquid; spoon sauce over ham.
Cook at **MEDIUM** 2 to 3 minutes, or until ham
is heated through.
Let stand, 3 minutes.

POLISH SAUSAGE (KIELBASA) WITH RED CABBAGE

2 pounds red cabbage, shredded
1 small apple, chopped
¼ cup sugar
¼ cup cider vinegar
1 tablespoon onion flakes
½ teaspoon caraway seeds
½ teaspoon salt
1¾ to 2 lb. Kielbasa sausage

Yield: 6 Servings

In 3-quart casserole, combine cabbage, apple,
sugar, vinegar, onion, caraway and salt. Cover
with glass lid. Cook at **HIGH** 7 to 9 minutes; stir
twice.
Meanwhile, score Kielbasa diagonally; arrange
on red cabbage. Cook, covered, at **HIGH** 14 to
15 minutes, or until heated through.
Let stand, covered, 5 minutes.

Lamb

MINT GLAZED LAMB

4 pound shank half leg of lamb
3 cloves garlic
2 teaspoons crushed rosemary
1/4 teaspoon pepper
1/2 cup mint jelly
1 can (8 1/2 oz.) pear slices, drained and mashed; reserve 1 tablespoon syrup

Yield: 8 Servings

Make 6 slits in lamb. Insert 1/3 clove garlic in each. Rub rosemary and pepper over lamb. In 10-inch square dish, place lamb fat side down on microwave roasting rack. In small glass bowl, combine remaining garlic, finely chopped, jelly and reserved syrup. Cook at **MEDIUM** 1 1/2 to 2 minutes or until melted; stir in pears. Spoon 1/3 mint glaze over lamb. Cover with wax paper. Cook at **MEDIUM** 9 to 11 minutes per pound for medium, or 12 to 14 1/2 minutes per pound for well. Halfway through cooking, turn meat over. Drain liquid and brush with glaze. Continue cooking. Brush with glaze. Let stand, covered, 15 minutes.

LAMB CURRY

1 pound boneless lamb, cut into 1 1/2-inch cubes
1 medium onion, chopped
1/4 cup butter or margarine, melted
3 tablespoons flour
1 can (10 3/4 oz.) chicken broth
1/3 cup raisins or peanuts
3 tablespoons lemon juice
1 to 1 1/2 tablespoons curry powder
1/2 teaspoon ginger
1/2 teaspoon salt
1/3 cup flaked coconut

Yield: 4 Servings

In 2-quart casserole, combine lamb, onion and butter. Cook 5 minutes; stir once. Stir in flour, broth, raisins, lemon juice, curry powder, ginger and salt. Cover with lid. Cook at **HIGH** 25 minutes, or until lamb is tender; stir twice. Sprinkle with coconut.
Let stand, covered, 5 minutes before serving over hot rice.

SHEPHERD'S PIE

1 medium onion, chopped
3 tablespoons butter or margarine
3 tablespoons flour
1 tablespoon chopped parsley
1 1/2 cups beef broth
2 cups cooked lamb or beef, cut into 3/4-inch cubes
1 package (10 oz.) frozen peas and carrots, thawed (see page 63)
1 1/2 to 2 cups hot mashed potatoes
Paprika

Yield: 4 Servings

Combine onion and butter in 2-quart casserole. Cook at **HIGH** 4 to 5 minutes, or until onion is tender. Stir in flour and parsley; gradually add broth. Cook at **HIGH** 6 to 7 minutes or until gravy is thickened; stir once. Stir in lamb, peas and carrots. Cook at **HIGH** 6 to 7 minutes, or until heated through; stir once. Spoon potatoes on top of casserole; sprinkle with paprika. Reheat, if necessary at **HIGH** 2 to 3 minutes.

IRISH STEW

2 pounds boneless lamb, cut into 1-inch cubes
2 medium carrots, cut into 1/4-inch slices
2 potatoes, peeled and cut into 1-inch cubes
2 1/2 cups water, divided
1 envelope (1 oz.) onion-mushroom soup mix
1 bay leaf
1/4 cup flour
1/2 teaspoon browning sauce

Yield: 8 Servings

In 4-quart casserole, arrange lamb, carrots and potatoes, forming three separate layers. In bowl, combine 2 cups water, onion-mushroom mix and bay leaf. Stir together until well blended. Pour mixture over potatoes. Cover with glass lid. Cook at **HIGH** 10 minutes and at **LOW** 1 to 1 1/4 hours, or until lamb and vegetables are tender; stir twice.
Blend flour with remaining 1/2 cup water and browning sauce; stir until smooth. Stir into dish. Cook at **HIGH** 4 to 6 minutes, or until stew is thickened; stir once.

DEFROSTING POULTRY AND GAME

- Poultry or game should be frozen in moisture and vapor proof wrapping materials.

- Cut-up chickens have better defrosting results, if pieces are frozen in a single layer.

- Remove poultry or game from original wrapper and set on a roasting rack or inverted microwave safe saucer placed in a dish.

- Set **DEFROST** and heat for time recommended in chart.

- Turn poultry or game two to four times during defrost.

- Shield ends of drumsticks, wings and breast bones on whole poultry, halfway through the defrost cycle.

- Break apart cut-up poultry, halfway through the defrost cycle. Remove small pieces such as wings, that may defrost before larger pieces.

- Rinse poultry or game under cold water to remove ice crystals.

- Estimate 10 minutes per pound defrosting time for poultry and game not listed on chart.

POULTRY	APPROX. DEFROSTING TIME (minutes per pound) at DEFROST

Chicken
  Whole
  Cut-up
  Boneless breasts
	12 to 14
	9 to 10
	12 to 14

Cornish hens Whole	12 to 16
Turkey Half	16 to 18

DIRECTIONS FOR ROASTING POULTRY

- Stuff bird, if desired; close cavity with cotton string or wooden toothpicks.

- Set poultry, cleaned and wiped dry, on a roasting rack placed in a dish.

- Season as desired, but salt after cooking.

- Browning sauce mixed with equal parts of butter will enhance appearance.

- Cook poultry (over 4 lbs.) breast-side down during first half of cooking.

- Loosely cover baking dish with wax paper to prevent spattering.

- If a large amount of juice accumulates in the bottom of baking dish, occasionally drain it. If desired, reserve for making gravy.

- Cover thin points (wings and legs) with strips of aluminum foil to prevent overcooking in these areas. Wooden toothpicks can be used to hold foil in place.

- Less tender chicken should be cooked in liquid (soup, broth, etc.) Use at least 1/4 cup liquid per pound of poultry.

- Use an oven cooking bag or covered casserole when cooking less tender chickens. Select a covered casserole deep enough so that the chicken does not touch the lid.

- If an oven cooking bag is used, prepare bag according to manufacturer's package directions. Do not use wire or metal twist-ties to close bag. Use nylon ties provided, otherwise use a piece of cotton string or a strip cut from the open end of the bag. Make six 1/2-inch slits in top of bag to allow steam to escape.

- Multiply the weight of the poultry by the minimum recommended minutes per pound. Program Power and Time.

- After cooking, check the internal temperature of the bird with a microwave or conventional meat thermometer, inserted into the thigh muscle. Check temperature in both muscles. The thermometer should not touch bone. If it does, the reading could be inaccurate.

- A thermometer cannot be accurately inserted into a small bird. To check doneness of a small bird, juices should be clear and the drumsticks should readily move up and down.
If the poultry is not cooked to the desired doneness, return it to oven and cook a few more minutes at the recommended power level.
DO NOT USE A CONVENTIONAL MEAT THERMOMETER IN THE MICROWAVE OVEN.

- Let stand, tented with foil, 10 to 15 minutes after heating. Stand time allows the temperature to equalize throughout the food and thereby finishes the cooking process.

For Poultry Parts
- Arrange pieces skin-side up in shallow baking dish, meatier portions toward edge of dish.

- Cover with wax paper or as recipe indicates to prevent spatter.

- Cook at **HIGH** 7 to 8 minutes per pound.

- Poultry is cooked when juices are clear (no pink color). If there is a slight pink color in the juice, return poultry parts to the oven and cook one or two minutes longer at the recommended power level.

- Let stand 5 minutes before serving or as recipe indicates.

POULTRY ROASTING CHART

POULTRY	POWER	APPROX. COOKING TIME (minutes per pound)	APPROXIMATE TEMPERATURE AFTER STANDING
Cornish Hens	HIGH	7½ to 8½	—
Chickens (up to 4 lb.)	HIGH	7½ to 9	—
Chickens (4 to 7 lb.)	MEDIUM	9½ to 10½	180° to 190°F
Turkey Breast	MEDIUM	12½ to 14½	180° to 190°F

Note: Check poultry with a conventional meat thermometer. If the poultry is not cooked to the desired temperature, return it to the oven and cook a few more minutes, at the recommended power level.

BARBECUED CHICKEN

2 pounds chicken parts
¾ cup barbecue sauce

Yield: 2—3 Servings

Arrange chicken, meatier portions toward edge of 8-inch square dish. Spread sauce evenly over chicken. Cook, covered with wax paper, at **HIGH** 16 to 18 minutes, or until chicken is tender. Halfway through cooking, baste chicken with sauce.
Let stand, covered, 5 minutes.

OVEN-CRISPY CHICKEN

6 chicken parts (2 lb.)
1 package (2⅜ oz.) seasoned coating mix for chicken

Yield: 3—4 Servings

Coat chicken with coating mix according to package directions. Arrange chicken, meatier portions toward edge of 8-inch square dish. Cover with wax paper. Cook at **HIGH** 16 to 18 minutes, or until done.
Let stand 5 minutes.

BUTTER BAKED CHICKEN

2 pounds chicken parts
2 tablespoons butter or margarine, melted
1/2 teaspoon browning sauce

Yield: 2—3 Servings

Arrange chicken, meatier portions toward edge of 8-inch square dish. Combine butter and browning sauce and brush half of mixture over chicken. Cook, covered with wax paper, at **HIGH** 16 to 18 minutes, or until chicken is tender. Halfway through cooking, brush remaining butter mixture on chicken. Let stand, covered, 5 minutes.

CHICKEN PARMESAN

1/4 cup water
1 egg
2 pound broiler-fryer, cut up
1 cup seasoned dry bread crumbs
1/2 cup grated Parmesan cheese
1/4 teaspoon paprika
2 tablespoons oil
1 can (8 oz.) tomato sauce or 1 cup
   spaghetti sauce
Oregano
1 cup (4 oz.) shredded mozzarella cheese

Yield: 4 Servings

Beat egg with water. Dip chicken in bread crumbs mixed with Parmesan cheese and paprika, then in egg and again in bread crumb mixture. Coat bottom of 8-inch square dish with 1 tablespoon oil. Place chicken in dish; sprinkle with remaining oil. Cook at **HIGH** 3 to 4 minutes; turn chicken and cook an additional 3 to 4 minutes. Top with tomato sauce and season with oregano. Cook at **HIGH** 10 to 12 minutes, or until sauce is hot. Sprinkle with mozzarella cheese and let stand, covered, 5 minutes or until cheese is melted.

CHICKEN CACCIATORE

1 1/2 pounds chicken parts
1 can (8 oz.) tomato sauce
1 jar (2 1/2 oz.) sliced mushrooms, drained
1 medium onion, chopped
1/2 tablespoon sugar, optional
1/2 teaspoon oregano
1/4 teaspoon finely chopped garlic
Dash pepper

Yield: 2—3 Servings

Arrange chicken, meatier portions toward edge of 8-inch square dish. Combine remaining ingredients and spoon over chicken. Cook, covered with wax paper, at **HIGH** 14 to 16 minutes, or until chicken is tender. Halfway through cooking, rearrange chicken. Let stand, covered, 5 minutes. Serve, if desired, with spaghetti.

HONEY GLAZED CHICKEN

2 chicken breasts, split
1/4 cup honey
2 tablespoons orange juice
1 tablespoon chili sauce
1 teaspoon prepared mustard
1 teaspoon browning sauce, optional

Yield: 4 Servings

Arrange chicken breasts, meatier portions toward edge of 8-inch square dish. In small bowl, combine honey, orange juice, chili sauce, mustard and browning sauce; stir well. Pour honey mixture over chicken. Cover with wax paper. Cook at **HIGH** 8 to 9 minutes and at **MEDIUM** 9 to 11 minutes or until chicken is tender. Let stand, uncovered, 5 minutes before serving.

HERB BAKED CHICKEN

1 teaspoon garlic salt
1 teaspoon paprika
½ teaspoon oregano
¼ teaspoon pepper
Juice and grated peel of 1 lemon
2 to 3 pound chicken, cut into serving pieces
1 jar (4½ oz.) sliced mushrooms, drained

Yield: 4 Servings

In small bowl, combine garlic, paprika, oregano, pepper and lemon peel; rub over chicken. Arrange chicken, meatier portions toward edge of 8-inch square dish. Drizzle with lemon and top with mushrooms. Cover with wax paper. Cook at **HIGH** 18 to 20 minutes or until chicken is tender.
Let stand, covered, 5 minutes before serving.

FIESTA CHICKEN ROLL-UPS

2 boneless chicken breasts (1 to 1¼ lb.), skinned, split and pounded thin
Chili powder
Pepper
½ cup (2 oz.) shredded Cheddar or Monterey jack cheese
4 teaspoons finely chopped jalapeno or green chili peppers
¼ cup butter or margarine, melted
¾ cup crushed taco or corn chips
1 can (8 oz.) taco or seasoned tomato sauce

Yield: 4 Servings

Season one side of each chicken with chili powder and pepper; sprinkle cheese and chopped peppers down center. Roll up jelly roll style; secure with wooden toothpicks. Carefully roll in melted butter, then crushed chips. Arrange seam-side down in 8-inch square dish. Cook, covered with wax paper, at **HIGH** 10 to 12 minutes, or until chicken is tender.
Let stand, covered, 5 minutes.
Meanwhile, in small glass bowl, cook taco sauce at **HIGH** 2 to 4 minutes, or until hot.
Serve over chicken.

CHICKEN IN WINE SAUCE

1 medium onion, sliced
¼ cup butter or margarine
2 boneless chicken breasts, skinned and thinly sliced (1 lb.)
Salt and pepper to taste
1 medium green pepper, cut into thin strips
⅓ cup white wine
1 jar (4½ oz.) sliced mushrooms, drained
2 tablespoons cornstarch
⅔ cup chicken broth

Yield: 4 Servings

Combine onion and butter in 8-inch square dish. Cook at **HIGH** 4 to 5 minutes, or until onion is tender; add chicken. Cook at **HIGH** 3 to 4 minutes; stir once. Season with salt and pepper; add green pepper and wine. Cover with plastic wrap. Cook at **HIGH** 3 to 4 minutes.
Add mushrooms. Blend cornstarch with broth; stir until smooth. Stir into dish.
Cook at **HIGH** 4 to 5 minutes, or until sauce is thickened; stir twice.

CALIFORNIA CHICKEN

2 chicken breasts, split (1¾ to 2 lb.)
2 teaspoons lemon juice
1 teaspoon onion flakes
Basil
Pepper
⅔ cup (2⅔ oz.) shredded Cheddar cheese
½ small avocado, thinly sliced
4 thin slices tomato

Yield: 4 Servings

Arrange chicken, meatier portions toward edge of 8-inch square dish. Sprinkle with lemon juice, onion flakes, basil and pepper. Cover with wax paper. Cook at **HIGH** 14 to 16 minutes, or until chicken is tender. Top chicken with ⅓ cup cheese, avocado, tomato and remaining cheese. Cover with wax paper. Cook at **HIGH** 3 to 4 minutes.
Let stand, covered, 5 minutes before serving.

CHICKEN TERIYAKI

2 pound broiler-fryer, cut-up
1 can (8 oz.) chunk pineapple in pineapple juice
1 clove garlic, finely chopped
¼ cup soy sauce
2 tablespoons packed brown sugar
½ teaspoon salt
¼ teaspoon ground ginger

Yield: 4–6 Servings

Arrange chicken, meatier portions toward the edge of 8-inch square dish. In small bowl, combine remaining ingredients; stir well. Pour sauce over chicken.
Cover with wax paper. Cook at **HIGH** 16 to 18 minutes, or until chicken is tender.
Let stand, covered, 5 minutes. To serve, spoon pineapple sauce over chicken.

HURRY CURRY CHICKEN

2 pounds chicken parts
1 can (10¾ oz.) condensed cream of chicken soup
1 tomato, cut into wedges, optional
½ cup raisins or peanuts
1 tablespoon curry powder
1 tablespoon onion flakes
⅛ teaspoon garlic powder

Yield: 4 Servings

Arrange chicken, meatier portions toward edge in 8-inch square dish. Combine remaining ingredients and pour evenly over chicken. Cook, covered with wax paper, at **HIGH** 16 to 18 minutes, or until chicken is tender.
Let stand, covered, 5 minutes; remove chicken to serving platter and stir sauce until smooth. Serve, if desired, with rice.

HAWAIIAN ISLAND CHICKEN

2 pounds chicken parts
2 tablespoons soy sauce
¼ teaspoon ginger
1 green pepper, cut into chunks
1 can (11 oz.) mandarin oranges, drained; reserve syrup
1 can (8¼ oz.) pineapple slices, drained and halved; reserve syrup
1 tablespoon cornstarch

Yield: 4 Servings

Arrange chicken in 8-inch square dish with meatier portions toward edge of dish. Brush with soy sauce blended with ginger. Add green pepper. Cook, covered with wax paper, at **HIGH** 14 to 16 minutes. Drain.
Let stand, covered, 5 minutes.
In 2-cup glass measure, blend cornstarch with one cup reserved syrup until smooth. Heat at **HIGH** 2 minutes, or until thickened. Stir once. Add fruit and pour over chicken; if necessary, reheat at **HIGH** 3 to 4 minutes.

CHICKEN LIVERS SUPREME

½ pound mushrooms, sliced
1 small onion, chopped
¼ cup butter or margarine
1 pound chicken livers, halved
2 to 3 tablespoons flour
1 teaspoon salt
½ teaspoon pepper
½ teaspoon thyme

Yield: 4 Servings

In 3-quart casserole, combine mushrooms, onion and butter. Cover with lid. Cook at **HIGH** 4 to 5 minutes, or until mushrooms and onions are tender; stir once.
Meanwhile, toss livers with flour. Stir in salt, pepper and thyme; cover. Cook at **HIGH** 10 to 11 minutes, or until livers are tender; stir twice.
Let stand, covered, 2 minutes. If desired, serve over rice.

SIMPLE CHICKEN POT PIE

2 cups cut-up cooked chicken
1 can (10¾ oz.) condensed cream of
    chicken soup
1 package (10 oz.) frozen mixed
    vegetables, defrosted (see page 63)
½ cup milk
⅛ teaspoon pepper
Dash Worcestershire sauce
2 cups seasoned croutons

Yield: 4 Servings

In 2-quart casserole, combine chicken, soup,
vegetables, milk, pepper and Worcestershire.
Cook at **HIGH** 8 to 9 minutes. Stir twice.
Crumble croutons over chicken mixture to form
a crust. Cook at **HIGH** 3 to 4 minutes.
Let stand 5 minutes before serving.

CHICKEN A LA KING

⅓ cup butter or margarine
2 tablespoons finely chopped green pepper
⅓ cup flour
1 teaspoon salt
⅛ teaspoon pepper
1¼ cups chicken broth
1¼ cups milk or half 'n half
3 cups cut-up cooked chicken or turkey
1 jar (4 oz.) sliced pimiento, drained
1 can (4 oz.) sliced mushrooms, drained
2 tablespoons dry sherry, optional

Yield: 6 Servings

Place butter and green pepper in 3-quart
casserole. Cook at **HIGH** 3 to 5 minutes, or until
green pepper is tender. Stir in flour, salt, and
pepper. Gradually add broth and milk; stir until
smooth. Cook at **MEDIUM** 8 to 10 minutes, or
until sauce is thickened; stir twice.
Add remaining ingredients. Cook at **MEDIUM** 7
to 9 minutes, or until heated through; stir twice.
Serve over toast, noodles or rice.

OPEN-FACED SANDWICHES WITH GRAVY

1 envelope (⅞ oz.) turkey gravy mix
1 cup water
4 slices white bread
½ pound sliced cooked turkey

Yield: 4 Servings

Combine gravy mix and water in 4-cup glass
measure. Cook at **HIGH** 3 to 4 minutes, or until
thickened; stir occasionally.
On paper plate, arrange turkey in four piles to fit
bread. Cook, covered, at **HIGH** 2 to 3 minutes
or until heated through. To serve, arrange
turkey on bread; top with gravy.

BRUNSWICK STEW

2½ to 3 pound chicken, cut into serving
    pieces
1¼ cups hot water, divided
10 whole peppercorns or pepper to taste
2 bay leaves, crushed
1 can (16 oz.) whole tomatoes, chopped
1 medium onion, thinly sliced
1 package (10 oz.) frozen succotash,
    defrosted (see page 63)
1 package (10 oz.) frozen sliced okra,
    defrosted (see page 63)
2 teaspoons salt
¼ cup flour

Yield: 4 Servings

In 3-quart casserole dish, combine chicken, 1
cup water, peppercorns and bay leaves. Cook,
covered with glass lid, at **HIGH** 7 to 9 minutes
and at **MEDIUM** 10 to 12 minutes, or until
chicken is tender. Strain and return broth to
dish; add tomatoes, onion, succotash, okra and
salt. Cook, covered, at **HIGH** 10 to 12 minutes;
stir once.
Meanwhile, remove chicken from bone. Blend
flour with remaining ¼ cup water; stir until
smooth. Stir chicken and water into stew. Cook,
covered, at **HIGH** 5 to 7 minutes, or until
thickened.

CORNISH HENS WITH PEACH SAUCE

2 cornish hens (1 lb. ea.), split
Browning sauce
Paprika
Pepper
1 can (16 oz.) sliced peaches in heavy syrup, drained; reserve 1/3 cup syrup
2/3 cup orange juice
1 tablespoon cornstarch
1/8 teaspoon ginger or cinnamon

Arrange hens, meatier portions toward edge of 8-inch square dish. Brush with browning sauce and season with paprika and pepper. Cook, covered with wax paper, at **HIGH** 11 to 14 minutes.
Let stand, covered, 5 minutes. Drain liquid from dish.
Meanwhile, in small glass bowl, combine reserved syrup, orange juice, cornstarch and ginger. Cook at **HIGH** 4 to 5 minutes, or until thickened; stir occasionally. Add peaches and spoon sauce over hens. If necessary, reheat at **HIGH** 2 to 3 minutes before serving.

TURKEY ROAST

2 pound frozen turkey roast

Yield: 6 Servings

Place turkey roast skin-side down in glass loaf dish. Cover with plastic wrap. Cook at **LOW** 25 minutes. Turn roast over; recover. Cook at **MEDIUM** 22 to 23 minutes or until roast registers 160°F when tested with a conventional meat thermometer. (Remove roast from oven before reading temperature).
Let stand, covered, 5 minutes before serving.

STUFFED CORNISH HENS WITH ORANGE HONEY SAUCE

1 1/2 cups hot water
1 cup orange juice
1 package (6 oz.) long grain and wild rice mix
2 slices bacon, cooked and crumbled (see page 33)
2 cornish hens (1 lb. ea.)
1/4 cup orange juice concentrate
1/4 cup honey
1/4 teaspoon browning sauce

Yield: 4 Servings

In 2-quart casserole, combine water, juice and rice. Cover with glass lid. Cook at **HIGH** 8 minutes and at **MEDIUM** 15 minutes, or until rice is tender; stir in bacon. Stuff hens with rice mixture; with string, tie wings to body of hen and legs together. Place hens in 8-inch square dish. Cover with wax paper. Cook at **HIGH** 18 to 20 minutes, or until hens are tender.
Meanwhile, combine remaining ingredients; brush hens every 5 minutes.
Let stand, covered, 10 minutes before serving. Meanwhile, cook remaining rice at **MEDIUM** 3 minutes; stir twice. Serve with hens.

TURKEY DIVAN

2 packages (10 oz. ea.) frozen broccoli spears, cooked and drained
2 to 3 cups cut-up cooked turkey or chicken
Salt and pepper to taste
1 can (11 oz.) condensed Cheddar cheese soup
1/2 cup milk
1/4 cup buttered bread crumbs
1/2 teaspoon paprika

Yield: 4 Servings

Arrange broccoli in 8-inch square dish. Top with turkey. Cook, covered with plastic wrap, at **HIGH** 4 to 5 minutes. Season with salt and pepper.
Combine soup and milk in small glass bowl; stir until smooth. Pour sauce over turkey. Cook, covered, at **MEDIUM** 6 to 7 minutes, or until heated through.
Let stand, covered, 5 minutes.
Top with bread crumbs mixed with paprika before serving.

TURKEY TETRAZZINI

¼ cup butter or margarine
¼ cup flour
1 teaspoon salt
¼ teaspoon pepper
1 cup chicken broth
1 cup half 'n half
4 cups cut-up cooked turkey or chicken
1 package (8 oz.) spaghetti, cooked and drained (see page 74)
1 can (4 oz.) sliced mushrooms, drained
2 tablespoons sherry, optional
¼ cup grated Parmesan cheese
Paprika

Yield: 6 Servings

Place butter in 3-quart casserole. Cook at **MEDIUM** 1½ minutes, or until melted. Stir in flour, salt and pepper. Gradually add broth and half 'n half; stir until smooth. Cook at **MEDIUM** 7 to 7½ minutes, or until sauce is thickened; stir twice. Stir in turkey, spaghetti, mushrooms and sherry. Cover with glass lid. Cook at **MEDIUM** 14 to 16 minutes, or until heated through. Stir; top with Parmesan cheese and paprika.
Let stand, covered, 5 minutes before serving.

BASIC BREAD STUFFING

5 stalks celery, thinly sliced
1 large onion, chopped
½ cup butter or margarine
8 cups fresh bread cubes
2 eggs
¼ cup water, optional
3 tablespoons parsley flakes
1 to 1½ teaspoons poultry seasoning
1 teaspoon salt
½ teaspoon pepper

Yield: 6—8 Servings, or enough to stuff
2 (2½ to 3 lb.) birds

In 3-quart casserole, combine celery, onion and butter. Cook at **HIGH** 7 to 9 minutes, or until celery and onion are tender; stir twice. Add remaining ingredients; combine thoroughly. Cook, covered with glass lid, at **MEDIUM** 5 to 6 minutes, or until heated through.

CONVENIENCE STUFFING MIXES

1½ to 1¾ cups hot water
¼ cup butter or margarine
1 package (6 to 6½ oz.) stuffing mix (chicken, cornbread, pork or rice varieties) with seasoning packet

Yield: 6 Servings or enough to stuff a 2½ to 3 pound chicken

In 2-quart casserole, heat water, butter and seasoning packet at **HIGH** 5 to 7 minutes; stir in stuffing crumbs.
Let stand, covered, 5 minutes before serving.

Variations: Add one of the following with seasoning packet:

1 cup chopped fresh cranberries or apple
½ cup raisins, chopped nuts, or chopped dried apricots
½ pound browned ground sausage, drained
1 can (8 oz.) whole kernel corn, drained

DEFROSTING FISH AND SEAFOOD

- Fish and seafood should be frozen in moisture and vapor proof wrapping materials.
- Small items such as scallops or shrimp should be frozen in a single layer.
- Remove fish from original wrapper and set on a roasting rack or invert a microwave safe saucer placed in a dish.
- Set **DEFROST** and heat for time recommended in chart.
- Turn whole fish or blocks of fillets over halfway through the defrost cycle.
- Separate shrimp or scallops halfway through the defrost cycle. Remove any pieces that are defrosted.
- Estimate 12 minutes per pound defrosting time for fish not listed below.

FISH	APPROX. DEFROSTING TIME (minutes per pound) at Power DEFROST
Crabmeat	30 to 32
Fish Fillets	8 to 12
Fish Steaks	10 to 12
Lobster Tails	12 to 14
Sea Scallops	16 to 20
Shrimp	12 to 14
Whole Fish	10 to 12

DIRECTIONS FOR PREPARING FISH AND SEAFOOD

- Use fresh or defrosted, cleaned fish.
- Arrange fish in a single layer in dish. For best results avoid overlapping edges as this will prevent fish from cooking evenly.
- Place thicker sections toward edge of the dish. (i.e. tail sections toward center).
- Arrange shrimp and scallops in a single layer in dish.
- Cook fish or seafood covered with plastic wrap.
- Rearrange or stir shrimp or scallops halfway through cooking.
- Cook according to directions given in chart.
- Test for doneness before adding extra cooking time. The color of seafood and fish should be opaque and the fish should flake easily when tested with a fork. If undercooked, return to oven and cook 15 to 30 seconds longer at recommended power level.
- Let stand, covered, 3 to 5 minutes before serving. Stand time allows the internal temperature to equalize throughout the food and thereby finishes the cooking process.

FISH AND SEAFOOD CHART

FISH OR SEAFOOD	AMOUNT	POWER	APPROX. COOKING TIME (in minutes)
Fish Fillets	1 lb.	HIGH	4$\frac{1}{2}$ to 6
Fish Steaks	4 (6 oz. ea.)	HIGH	5$\frac{1}{2}$ to 7
Sea Scallops	1 lb.	MEDIUM	6 to 7$\frac{1}{2}$
Shrimp medium size (shelled and cleaned)	1 lb.	MEDIUM	4$\frac{1}{2}$ to 6
Whole fish (stuffed or unstuffed)	1$\frac{1}{2}$ to 1$\frac{3}{4}$ lb.	HIGH	8 to 10

STUFFED FLOUNDER CUPS

1 onion, chopped
1/4 pound mushrooms, sliced
3 tablespoons butter
1 teaspoon thyme
1/4 teaspoon salt
5 slices bread, cubed
1 egg, beaten
2 tablespoons chopped parsley
4 large flounder fillets (1 1/2 lb.)
Hollandaise sauce

Yield: 4 Servings

In medium bowl, combine onion, mushrooms, butter, thyme and salt. Cook at **HIGH** 4 to 5 minutes, or until onion is tender. Stir in bread, egg, and parsley. Grease four 6 ounce custard cups. Add fillets, allowing ends to extend over edges. Spoon stuffing into fillets. Fold fish to enclose stuffing. Place cups in a circle. Cover with plastic wrap. Cook at **HIGH** 7 to 10 minutes, or until fish flakes when tested with a fork.
If desired, serve with Hollandaise sauce.

PARCHMENT SEAFOOD SPECTACULAR

2 halibut or other seafood steaks
  (6 to 8 oz. ea.)
1 tablespoon brandy
1/2 tablespoon lemon juice
1 tablespoon butter or margarine
1 tablespoon dried chives
Salt and pepper to taste
1/2 cup (1 oz.) sliced fresh mushrooms
1 small apple, thinly sliced

Yield: 2 Servings

For each serving, place fish on 10" × 15" piece parchment paper. Combine brandy and lemon juice; brush on fish. Dot each with butter, chives and season with salt and pepper. Mound mushrooms and apple on top; bring paper up around fish. Fold edges over twice to seal top; fold side edges up. Place on glass tray. Cook at **HIGH** 7 to 9 minutes.
Let stand, 3 minutes. Serve packet directly on dinner plate.

FILLET AMANDINE

3 tablespoons butter or margarine
3 tablespoons slivered almonds
1/2 pound fish fillets
Salt and pepper to taste
Lemon juice
Parsley flakes

Yield: 2 Servings

Place butter and almonds in 8-inch square dish. Cook at **HIGH** 3 to 4 minutes; stir once. Dip fillets in butter and arrange in same dish; spoon almonds and butter on top of fish. Season with salt and pepper. Sprinkle with lemon juice. Cover with plastic wrap. Cook at **HIGH** 4 to 5 minutes, or until fish flakes when tested with a fork.
Let stand, covered, 3 minutes; sprinkle with parsley before serving.

FILLET PROVENÇALE

1 medium onion, sliced
2 tablespoons butter or margarine
1 clove garlic, finely chopped
1 can (16 oz.) stewed tomatoes, chopped
1 jar (4 1/2 oz.) sliced mushrooms, drained
1/4 cup white wine
1/4 teaspoon basil
6 flounder fillets (about 1/4 lb. ea.)
Salt

Yield: 6 Servings

In 8-inch square dish, combine onion, butter and garlic. Cover with plastic wrap. Cook at **HIGH** 3 to 4 minutes. Stir in tomatoes, mushrooms, wine and basil. Cook, covered, at **HIGH** 4 minutes and at **MEDIUM** 3 to 5 minutes. Meanwhile, season fish with salt, skin side only. Roll up (skin-side in) and arrange seam-side down in sauce by edge of dish. Spoon sauce over fish. Cook, covered, at **HIGH** 5 to 6 minutes, or until fish flakes when tested with a fork.
Let stand, covered, 5 minutes.

SALMON RING WITH CUCUMBER SAUCE

2 eggs, slightly beaten
1 can (16 oz.) salmon, drained and flaked
1 cup dry bread crumbs
½ cup milk
1 stalk celery, chopped
2 tablespoons chopped green pepper
2 tablespoons chopped green onion
1 tablespoon lemon juice
½ teaspoon salt

Cucumber Sauce:
½ cup chopped cucumber
½ cup sour cream
2 tablespoons chopped green onion
2 tablespoons milk

Yield: 4 Servings

In medium bowl, combine egg, salmon, bread crumbs, milk, celery, green pepper, onion, lemon juice and salt; mix well. Spoon into a 2-quart ring mold. Cover with wax paper. Cook at **HIGH** 5 minutes and at **MEDIUM** 4 to 5 minutes, or until heated through.
Let stand, uncovered, 5 minutes. Loosen edges with spatula before unmolding. Combine all ingredients for cucumber sauce in small bowl. Stir well; spoon over unmolded salmon ring.

FISHERMAN'S POT

1 can (28 oz.) whole tomatoes, chopped
1 cup chicken broth
3 stalks celery, thinly sliced
1 medium onion, sliced
1 tablespoon sugar, optional
1 bay leaf
1 tablespoon chopped parsley
1 teaspoon salt
½ teaspoon finely chopped garlic
Dash thyme
1 pound fish fillets, cut into 2-inch chunks
¼ cup white wine, optional

Yield: 4 Servings

In 3-quart casserole, combine tomatoes, broth, celery, onion, sugar, bay leaf, parsley, salt, garlic and thyme. Cover with glass lid. Cook at **HIGH** 8 minutes and at **MEDIUM** 10 minutes; stir once. Add fish and wine; recover. Cook at **MEDIUM** 7 to 8 minutes, or until fish flakes when tested with a fork; stir once.
Let stand, covered, 3 minutes before serving.

PARTY TUNA CASSEROLE

2 tablespoons butter or margarine, melted
1 tablespoon soy sauce
1 teaspoon garlic powder
1 can (3 oz.) chow mein noodles
1 can (10¾ oz.) condensed cream of mushroom soup
1 can (7 oz.) tuna, drained and flaked
3 stalks celery, finely chopped
¼ pound salted cashew nuts
2 tablespoons onion flakes
¼ cup water

Yield: 4 Servings

Combine butter, soy sauce, garlic and noodles; toss well and reserve. In 8-inch round dish, combine soup, tuna, celery, nuts, onion and water. Cook at **HIGH** 7 to 8 minutes, or until heated through; stir twice. Top with noodles. Cook at **HIGH** 1 minute.
Let stand, covered, 5 minutes.

TUNA TEMPTER

1 can (7 oz.) tuna, drained and flaked
⅓ cup mayonnaise
Celery seed
Onion powder
Salt and pepper
4 slices whole wheat bread, toasted
4 thin slices tomato
4 slices American cheese

Yield: 4 Servings

Combine tuna and mayonnaise; season with celery seed, onion, salt and pepper. Spread tuna on toast; top with tomato. Place on paper plate. Cook sandwiches at **MEDIUM** 2½ to 3 minutes; top with cheese. Cook at **MEDIUM** 2 to 3 minutes, or until cheese is melted.

SEAFARER'S SANDWICH

1 package (8 oz.) frozen fried fish fillets (4 fillets)
4 slices American cheese
4 hamburger rolls
4 tablespoons tartar sauce or cocktail sauce

Yield: 4 Sandwiches

Place fillets on paper plate. Cook at **HIGH** 4 to 5 minutes. Top with cheese. Cook at **MEDIUM** 2 to 2½ minutes, or until cheese is melted. Place fillet in roll; top with tartar sauce.

SHRIMP CREOLE

3 stalks celery, finely chopped
1 green pepper, finely chopped
1 large onion, finely chopped
2 tablespoons oil
2 cloves garlic, finely chopped
1 can (15 oz.) tomato sauce
1½ pounds medium shrimp, shelled and
    cleaned
1 teaspoon salt
¼ teaspoon pepper
¼ to ½ teaspoon hot pepper sauce

Yield: 4 Servings

In 2-quart casserole, combine celery, green
pepper, onion, oil and garlic. Cook at **HIGH** 7 to
8 minutes, or until vegetables are tender. Stir in
remaining ingredients. Cover with glass lid.
Cook at **HIGH** 4 minutes and at **MEDIUM** 6 to
7 minutes, or until shrimp is tender; stir once.
Let stand, covered, 3 minutes before serving.

SHRIMP SCAMPI

½ cup butter or margarine
2 cloves garlic, finely chopped
2 tablespoons lemon juice
2 tablespoons chopped parsley
½ teaspoon salt
1½ pounds medium shrimp, shelled and
    cleaned
Paprika

Yield: 4 Servings

Place butter and garlic in 8-inch round dish.
Cook at **HIGH** 2 to 2½ minutes, or until butter
is melted. Add lemon juice, parsley and salt; stir
in shrimp. Cover with plastic wrap. Cook at
MEDIUM 5½ to 6½ minutes, or until shrimp is
tender; stir once.
Let stand, covered, 5 minutes; sprinkle with
paprika before serving.

CLAMS-STEAMER STYLE

12 littlenecks or cherrystone clams,
    scrubbed
¼ cup hot water

Yield: 12 Clams

Place clams and water in 8-inch square dish.
Cover completely with plastic wrap. Do not vent
plastic. Cook at **HIGH** 5 to 7 minutes, or until
clams open. Remove clams from dish as they
open to prevent overcooking.
Serve, if desired, with melted butter and cocktail
sauce.

SIMPLE SEAFOOD NEWBURG

1 can (10¾ oz.) condensed cream of
    mushroom soup
1 package (10 oz.) frozen peas, defrosted
¼ cup milk or half 'n half
1 pound seafood, cooked (see page 56) and
    cut into bite-sized pieces
1 jar (2½ oz.) sliced mushrooms, drained
2 to 3 tablespoons sherry

Yield: 4 Servings

In 1½-quart casserole, combine soup, peas and
milk. Cover with lid. Cook at **HIGH** 5 to 6
minutes; stir once.
Add remaining ingredients; cover. Cook at
HIGH 4 to 5 minutes, or until heated through;
stir once.
Let stand, covered, 3 minutes before serving.

MARYLAND CRAB BAKE

4 stalks celery, chopped
2 green peppers, chopped
2 medium onions, chopped
3 tablespoons butter or margarine
1 cup mayonnaise
4 hard-cooked eggs, chopped (see page 71)
2 packages (6 oz. ea.) crabmeat, drained
    and flaked
1 teaspoon Worcestershire sauce
½ teaspoon pepper
½ teaspoon salt
1 cup buttery cracker crumbs
2 tablespoons butter or margarine, melted
Dash paprika

Yield: 4–6 Servings

In 2-quart casserole, combine celery, green
pepper, onion and 3 tablespoons butter. Cover
with glass lid. Cook at **HIGH** 6 to 7 minutes, or
until vegetables are tender; stir once. Drain. Stir
in mayonnaise, eggs, crab, Worcestershire,
pepper and salt. Cook, covered, at **MEDIUM** 7
to 9 minutes, or until heated through; stir twice.
Combine cracker crumbs, melted butter and
paprika; sprinkle over casserole.
Let stand 5 minutes before serving.

COQUILLE ST. JACQUES

¼ cup white wine
1 pound sea scallops
2 tablespoons butter or margarine
1 tablespoon onion flakes
2 tablespoons flour
¼ teaspoon salt
Dash white pepper
¾ cup milk or half 'n half
1 jar (2½ oz.) sliced mushrooms, drained
⅓ cup (1⅓ oz.) shredded Swiss cheese
¼ cup buttered bread crumbs
Parsley, chopped

Yield: 4 Servings

Place scallops in 8-inch round dish. Pour wine over scallops; cover with plastic wrap. Cook at **MEDIUM** 5 to 6 minutes or until scallops are tender; stir once. Drain liquid and reserve ¼ cup; let scallops stand, covered.
Place butter and onion in medium bowl. Cook at **HIGH** 1 minute. Stir in flour, salt and pepper. Gradually add milk and reserved liquid; stir until smooth. Cook at **MEDIUM** 4 to 5 minutes, or until mixture is thickened; stir twice. Stir in mushrooms and cheese; add scallops. Spoon mixture into 4 individual glass ramekins or serving dishes; top with bread crumbs and parsley. Arrange ramekins in oven. Cook at **MEDIUM** 2 to 3 minutes, or until heated through.

SCALLOPS WITH HERB LEMON BUTTER

¼ cup butter or margarine
½ teaspoon basil
½ teaspoon crushed rosemary
½ teaspoon salt
1 pound sea scallops
Juice from 1 lemon
Paprika

Yield: 4 Servings

In 8-inch round dish, combine butter, basil, rosemary and salt. Cook at **HIGH** 1½ minutes, or until melted. Stir in scallops and sprinkle with lemon juice; spoon butter mixture over scallops. Cover with plastic wrap. Cook at **MEDIUM** 5 to 7 minutes, or until scallops are opaque and tender; stir once. Sprinkle with paprika. Let stand, covered, 5 minutes before serving.

STUFFED LOBSTER TAILS

2 lobster tails (8 oz. ea.)
1½ tablespoons butter or margarine, melted
2½ tablespoons seasoned dry bread crumbs
Pinch each onion powder, paprika, salt

Lemon Butter:
½ cup butter
1 to 2 tablespoons lemon juice

Yield: 2 Servings

With kitchen shears, cut both sides of the soft shell (underneath) of the lobster, from edge to the tail. Remove soft shell. Arrange in glass pie plate, flesh-side up and tails toward center. Combine remaining ingredients; sprinkle over lobster. Cover with wax paper. Cook at **MEDIUM** 6½ to 7½ minutes, or until lobster flakes when tested with a fork.
Let stand 3 minutes.
Combine butter and lemon juice in small glass bowl. Cook at **MEDIUM** 2 to 3 minutes or until butter is melted. Stir well.

Vegetables

DIRECTIONS FOR COOKING FROZEN VEGETABLES

Frozen Vegetables

- Remove vegetables from their package and place in a 1 or 1½-quart covered casserole.
- Add amount of water recommended in chart.
- Cover with lid.
- Cook according to time given in chart.
- Stir two-thirds the way through cooking.
- Stir; let stand, covered, 2 minutes before serving.

Frozen Vegetables in a Pouch

- Remove pouch from package and place on a microwave safe plate.
- Pierce one hole in pouch with a long handled fork.
- Cook 5 to 7 minutes.
- Rotate dish ¼ turn two-thirds the way through cooking.
- Let stand 2 minutes before serving.
- Use scissors to cut package open.

Frozen Corn on the Cob

- Place frozen corn in a square or oblong dish.
- Cover with plastic wrap.
- Cook according to time given in chart.
- Rearrange and turn corn over two-thirds the way through cooking.
- Let stand, covered, 2 minutes before serving.

DIRECTIONS FOR COOKING CANNED VEGETABLES

- Empty contents of can into a microwave safe serving dish or casserole.
- Stir occasionally during heating.
- Heat an 8 oz. can of vegetables 2 to 3 minutes.
- Heat a 16 to 17 oz. can of vegetables 3 to 4 minutes.
- Let stand, uncovered, 2 minutes before serving.

DIRECTIONS FOR COOKING FRESH VEGETABLES

- Weights given in the chart for fresh vegetables are the purchase weights before peeling and trimming.
- Prepare vegetables for cooking. Cut into size recommended in chart.
- Place vegetables in casserole dish. Add amount of water recommended in chart. Add salt to water or salt after cooking. Cover with lid or plastic wrap.
- Whole vegetables, such as, potatoes, eggplant or acorn squash should be pierced with a fork several times before cooking. Arrange on a paper towel in oven. Arrange potatoes in a circular pattern on paper towel.
- Cook according to time recommended in chart. Two-thirds the way through cooking, stir, rearrange and/or turn vegetables over.
- Let stand, covered, before serving. Whole vegetables should stand 5 minutes.
- Vegetables that are cut into pieces should stand 2 minutes.

FRESH AND FROZEN VEGETABLE CHART

VEGETABLE	AMOUNT	WATER	APPROX. COOKING TIME (in minutes) at HIGH
Artichokes Fresh, 6 to 8 oz. ea.	1	1 tablespoon	4 to 5
	2	2 tablespoons	6 to 7
	4	¼ cup	8 to 9
Frozen hearts	1 pkg. (9 oz.)	2 tablespoons	7 to 8
Asparagus Fresh, 6-in. spears	1 lb.	2 tablespoons	5 to 6
Frozen, spears	1 pkg. (10 oz.)	—	7 to 8
Beans, Green or Wax Fresh, cut into 1½-in. pieces	1 lb.	¼ cup	8 to 10
Frozen	1 pkg. (9 oz.)	—	7 to 8
Broccoli Fresh, cut into spears	1 lb.	2 tablespoons	5 to 7
Frozen, chopped	1 pkg. (10 oz.)	—	7 to 8
spears	1 pkg. (10 oz.)	—	7 to 8
Brussel Sprouts Fresh	1 tub (10 oz.)	¼ cup	7 to 8
Frozen	1 pkg. (10 oz.)	2 tablespoons	7 to 8
Cabbage Fresh, shredded	4 cups	¼ cup	9 to 10
Carrots Fresh, sliced ¼-in. thick	1 lb.	¼ cup	8 to 9
Frozen	1 pkg. (10 oz.)	—	6 to 7

VEGETABLE	AMOUNT	WATER	APPROX. COOKING TIME (in minutes) at HIGH
Cauliflower			
Fresh, cut into flowerets	1 lb.	$1/4$ cup	6 to 7
whole	$1^1/2$ to $1^3/4$ lb.	$1/4$ cup	12 to 14
Frozen, flowerets	1 pkg. (10 oz.)	—	6 to 7
Corn			
Fresh on the Cob	1 ear	2 tablespoons	4 to $4^1/2$
	2 ears	2 tablespoons	6 to 7
	4 ears	$1/4$ cup	8 to 9
Frozen on the Cob	1 ear	—	4 to 5
	2 ears	—	6 to 8
	4 ears	—	12 to 14
Frozen, Whole Kernels	1 pkg. (10 oz.)	—	7 to 8
Eggplant			
Fresh, cubed	$1^1/2$ lb.	2 tablespoons	9 to 10
whole, pierce skin	$1^1/4$ lb. to $1^1/2$ lb.	—	8 to 9
Lima Beans			
Frozen	1 pkg. (10 oz.) Plus 1 tablespoon butter or margarine	$1/2$ cup — —	10 to 12
Mixed Vegetables			
Frozen	1 pkg. (10 oz.)	—	7 to 8
Okra			
Frozen, sliced	1 pkg. (10 oz.)	2 tablespoons	8 to 9
whole	1 pkg. (10 oz.)	2 tablespoons	9 to 10
Onions			
Fresh, small whole	8 to 10 (1 lb.)	$1/4$ cup	7 to 8
Peas, Green			
Fresh	2 cups, shelled	2 tablespoons	6 to 7
Frozen	1 pkg. (10 oz.)		7 to 8
Peas, Snow			
Frozen	1 pkg. (6 oz.)	—	4 to 5
Potatoes			
Fresh, (6 to 8 oz. ea.)	1	—	4 to 5
	2	—	9 to 10
	3	—	10 to 12
	4	—	12 to 14
Spinach			
Fresh, leaf	1 bag (10 oz.)	—	4 to 5
Frozen, leaf or chopped	1 pkg. (10 oz.)	—	7 to 8
Squash, Summer			
Fresh, sliced $1/4$-in. thick	1 lb.	1 tablespoon	6 to 7
Frozen	1 package (10 oz.)	—	6 to 7
Squash, Winter			
Fresh, whole about 1 lb. ea.	1	—	6 to 7
	2	—	9 to 11
Frozen, whipped	1 pkg. (12 oz.)	—	8 to 9

PREPARING DRIED BEANS AND PEAS

- Combine hot tap water, beans/peas and 2 tablespoons oil in casserole.
- Cover dish with casserole lid.
- Bring beans and hot water to a boil at HIGH.
- Let beans soak, covered, 1 hour.
- Bring beans or black-eyed peas in water to a boil at HIGH.

- Cook at MEDIUM until tender.
- Stir twice during cooking.
- Split peas and lentils do not require soak period. Boil water and cook at MEDIUM.

ITEM	CONTAINER	AMOUNT OF HOT WATER	APPROX. COOKING TIME (in minutes)	
			To Boil Water at HIGH	To Cook Beans at MEDIUM
Black-eyed peas (1 lb.)	5-quart casserole	2½ quarts	20 to 22	25 to 30
Kidney beans, Lima beans (small) or Northern beans (1 lb.)	5-quart casserole	2 quarts	18 to 20	40 to 45
Lima beans (large) (1 lb.)	5-quart casserole	2½ quarts	20 to 22	35 to 40
Split peas or Lentils (1 lb.)	3-quart casserole	1½ quarts	14 to 16	25 to 30

VEGETARIAN ASPARAGUS DELIGHT

Water
1 can (16 oz.) asparagus spears, drained;
   reserve liquid
1 can (3 oz.) sliced mushrooms, drained;
   reserve liquid
1 package (1¼ oz.) cheese sauce mix
1 tablespoon onion flakes
1 hard-cooked egg, chopped (see page 71)
¼ cup (1 oz.) shredded Cheddar cheese
2 tablespoons slivered almonds
Paprika

Yield: 2 Servings

In 2-cup glass measure, add enough water to reserved liquids to equal 1 cup. Stir in cheese sauce mix and onion. Cook at **HIGH** 3 to 3½ minutes, or until thickened; stir occasionally. Add mushrooms, egg and shredded cheese. Arrange asparagus in 9″ × 5″ × 3″ loaf dish. Pour on cheese mixture. Sprinkle with almonds and paprika. Cook, covered with wax paper, at **HIGH** 4 to 5 minutes or until bubbly.
Let stand 5 minutes before serving.

ARTICHOKES FOR TWO

8 tablespoons butter or margarine, melted,
   divided
½ teaspoon garlic salt
2 fresh artichokes (8 oz. ea.)
1 lemon, thinly sliced and halved
¼ cup dry seasoned bread crumbs
2 tablespoons grated Parmesan cheese
¼ teaspoon paprika
¼ teaspoon parsley

Yield: 2 Servings

Combine 6 tablespoons butter with garlic in small bowl. Set aside. Cut stem off artichokes; trim tips of leaves; rinse. Place lemon in between leaves; arrange artichokes in 1½-quart casserole. Pour butter mixture over artichokes. Cover with plastic wrap. Cook at **HIGH** 14 to 16 minutes. Combine 2 tablespoons butter with remaining ingredients. Sprinkle over cooked artichokes.
Let stand, covered, 5 minutes before serving.

APPLE BAKED SQUASH

1 medium butternut squash, halved
   lengthwise, peeled and seeded
1 medium apple, quartered, peeled, and
   seeded
¼ cup packed brown sugar
¼ cup butter or margarine, softened
1½ teaspoons flour
½ teaspoon salt
¼ teaspoon cinnamon

Yield: 4 Servings

Cut squash into ½-inch slices. Arrange slices in 8-inch square dish. Cut apple into thin slices; place on top of squash.
Combine remaining ingredients until well blended in small bowl. Drop by spoonfuls over apple squash mixture. Cover with plastic wrap. Cook at **HIGH** 17 to 18 minutes or until tender. Let stand, covered, 5 minutes before serving.

HONEY ACORN SQUASH

2 acorn squash (¾ lb. ea.)
4 tablespoons honey
4 teaspoons butter or margarine
⅛ teaspoon grated lemon peel

Yield: 4 Servings

Pierce skin of squash several times. Place on a paper towel in oven. Cook at **HIGH** 5 to 7 minutes.
Let stand 3 minutes.
Cut squash in half; scoop out seeds. Arrange squash, cut-side up in 8-inch square dish. Top with honey, butter and lemon. Cook, covered with plastic wrap, at **HIGH** 7½ to 9 minutes or until squash is tender.
Let stand, covered, 2 minutes before serving.

GREEN BEANS AMANDINE

¼ cup slivered almonds
3 tablespoons butter or margarine
1¼ to 1½ pounds fresh green beans, cut into 1½-inch pieces
¼ cup water
½ teaspoon salt
Dash nutmeg, optional

Yield: 4 Servings

Combine almonds and butter in glass measure. Cook at **HIGH** 3 to 4 minutes, or until almonds are lightly browned; reserve.
Combine beans and water in 2-quart casserole. Cook, covered with glass lid, at **HIGH** 10 to 12 minutes, or until beans are tender; stir once. Add remaining ingredients, almonds and butter. Let stand, covered, 5 minutes before serving.

CARAWAY CABBAGE

¼ cup butter or margarine
1½ pound cabbage, cut into 4-wedges
¼ teaspoon caraway seeds
¼ cup water

Yield: 4 Servings

Place butter in 8-inch square dish. Cook at **MEDIUM** 1 minute or until melted. Brush cabbage with butter and arrange, wide edge towards rim, in same dish. Sprinkle with caraway and water. Cook, covered with plastic wrap, at **HIGH** 10 to 12 minutes or until cabbage is almost tender.
Let stand, covered, 5 minutes before serving.

CLASSIC COMPANY GREEN BEANS

2 cans (16 oz. ea.) french-cut green beans, drained; reserve ¼ cup liquid
1 can (10¾ oz.) condensed cream of mushroom soup
1 can (3 oz.) french fried onions

Yield: 6 Servings

Combine beans, reserved liquid and soup in 2-quart casserole. Cook, covered with glass lid, at **HIGH** 6 to 8 minutes. Stir occasionally. Top with onion pieces. Reheat, uncovered, at **HIGH** 1 to 2 minutes or until hot.

BETTER BAKED BEANS

3 slices bacon, diced
1 green pepper, chopped or 1 medium onion, chopped
2 cans (16 oz. ea.) pork and beans, drained
¼ cup molasses
¼ cup catsup
1 tablespoon prepared mustard
½ teaspoon Worcestershire sauce
Dash hot pepper sauce

Yield: 6 Servings

Combine bacon and green pepper in 1½-quart casserole. Cook at **HIGH** 4 to 5 minutes, or until bacon is crisp; stir once. Stir in remaining ingredients. Cook, covered with wax paper, at **HIGH** 5 to 6 minutes and at **MEDIUM** 6 to 8 minutes; stir twice.

CALICO CORN RELISH

2 cans (16 oz. ea.) whole kernel corn, drained; reserve liquid
3 stalks celery, chopped
1 green pepper, diced
1 small onion, finely chopped
2 to 3 tablespoons sugar
1 tablespoon cornstarch
⅓ cup cider vinegar
2 tablespoons diced pimiento

Yield: 6 Servings

Measure reserved corn liquid to equal 1¼ cups. In 2½-quart bowl, combine liquid, corn, celery, green pepper, onion and sugar. Cook at **HIGH** 4 to 6 minutes; stir once. Stir in cornstarch blended with vinegar. Cook at **HIGH** 3 to 5 minutes or until slightly thickened; stir occasionally. Add pimento. Relish thickens more upon standing. Chill before serving.

ORANGE GLAZED CARROTS

1 pound carrots, thinly sliced
3 tablespoons honey or packed brown sugar
3 tablespoons orange juice
½ teaspoon grated orange or lemon peel

Yield: 4 Servings

Combine all ingredients in 1-quart casserole. Cook, covered with plastic wrap, at **HIGH** 7 to 9 minutes, or until carrots are tender; stir twice. Let stand, covered, 5 minutes before serving.

RATATOUILLE

2 medium onions, sliced
1 medium green pepper, sliced
1/3 cup oil
2 cloves garlic, finely chopped
1 medium eggplant (about 1 1/2 lb.), peeled
 and cut into 1/2-inch pieces
3 medium tomatoes (about 1 lb.), chopped
2 medium zucchini (about 1 lb.), thinly
 sliced
1/4 cup vegetable juice cocktail or tomato
 juice
2 teaspoons each basil and parsley flakes
1 teaspoon salt
1/4 teaspoon pepper

Yield: 8 Servings

In 5-quart casserole, combine onions, green
pepper, oil and garlic. Cover with glass lid. Cook
at **HIGH** 5 to 6 minutes; stir once. Stir in
remaining ingredients; cover. Cook at **HIGH** 20
to 22 minutes; stir twice. Let stand, covered, 5
minutes before serving.

*Variation: Add 1/4 pound fresh mushrooms,
sliced or 1 can (4 oz.) sliced mushrooms,
drained with eggplant.*

CHEESY VEGETABLE
CASSEROLE

4 medium onions, sliced (1 lb.)
1 teaspoon salt
1/2 teaspoon basil
1/4 teaspoon pepper
3 tablespoons butter or margarine
1/2 cup dry seasoned bread crumbs
Paprika
4 medium tomatoes, (1 1/2 lb.), sliced
6 slices American cheese (1 oz. ea.)

Yield: 6 Servings

Place onions in medium glass bowl. Cook,
covered with plastic wrap, at **HIGH** 5 1/2 to 6 1/2
minutes; stir once. Stir in salt, basil and pepper.
Place butter in small glass bowl. Cook at
MEDIUM 1 minute, or until melted. Stir in
bread crumbs and paprika. In 2-quart casserole,
alternately layer half the tomatoes, onions and
cheese; top with remaining tomatoes and
onions. Cover with plastic wrap. Cook at **HIGH**
12 to 14 minutes. Top with remaining cheese,
then bread crumb mixture.
Let stand, covered, 5 minutes before serving.

GARDEN SUCCOTASH

1 package (10 oz.) frozen lima beans
1 package (10 oz.) frozen whole kernel
 corn
2 tablespoons chopped pimiento, optional
1/4 cup milk or half 'n half
3 tablespoons butter or margarine
1/2 teaspoon salt
Dash pepper

Yield: 6 Servings

In 2-quart casserole, combine lima beans, corn
and pimento. Cook, covered with glass lid, at
HIGH 9 to 11 minutes, or until vegetables are
tender. Stir once. Stir in remaining ingredients.
Cook, covered, at **HIGH** 2 to 3 minutes, or until
heated through.

ZUCCHINI PARMESAN

4 medium zucchini, sliced into 1-inch pieces
 (1 1/2 lb.)
1/4 cup grated Parmesan cheese
1 can (8 oz.) tomato sauce
1/2 cup (2 oz.) shredded mozzarella cheese

Yield: 4 Servings

In 8-inch round dish, combine zucchini, cheese,
and tomato sauce. Cover with plastic wrap.
Cook at **HIGH** 10 to 12 minutes or until zucchini
is tender; stir once. Sprinkle with mozzarella
cheese.
Let stand, covered, 5 minutes before serving.

MASHED POTATOES

6 medium potatoes (2 lb.), peeled and
  quartered
1/4 to 3/4 cup milk
1/4 cup butter or margarine
Salt and pepper to taste

Yield: 6 Servings

Rinse potatoes; drain. Place potatoes in medium glass bowl. Cook at **HIGH** 13 to 15 minutes, or until tender. Stir once.
Let stand, covered, 5 minutes; drain.
Meanwhile, combine remaining ingredients in small glass bowl. Cook at **HIGH** 3 to 4 minutes or until hot. Add to potatoes and mash until smooth.

BAKED STUFFED POTATOES

4 medium potatoes, baked (see page 63)
1/2 cup (2 oz.) shredded Cheddar cheese
1/3 to 1/2 cup milk
2 tablespoons butter or margarine
1 egg
Salt and pepper to taste
Paprika

Yield: 4 Servings

Cut a thin slice, lengthwise, from each potato. Gently scoop out potato leaving thin shell. Combine potato, cheese, milk, butter, egg, salt and pepper; mash until smooth. Spoon potato mixture into shells and sprinkle with paprika. Arrange in spoke-like fashion on paper towel in oven. Cook at **HIGH** 8 to 10 minutes, or until hot.

BUTTERED CRUMB POTATOES

4 small potatoes, peeled
2 tablespoons butter or margarine, melted
1/2 cup seasoned dry bread crumbs

Yield: 4 Servings

Roll potatoes in butter, then in bread crumbs. Arrange in 8-inch dish; drizzle with remaining butter. Cook, covered with wax paper, at **HIGH** 10 to 12 minutes or until potatoes are tender. Let stand, covered, 3 minutes before serving.

HOT GERMAN POTATO SALAD

4 slices bacon, diced
1 small onion, finely chopped
2 teaspoons flour
1/3 cup cider vinegar
2 tablespoons packed brown sugar
1/2 teaspoon celery seed
Salt and pepper to taste
4 medium potatoes, baked, (see page 63),
  peeled and sliced

Yield: 4 Servings

Combine bacon and onion in 8-inch round dish. Cook at **HIGH** 3 to 5 minutes; stir occasionally. Stir in flour, vinegar, sugar, celery seed, salt and pepper. Cook at **HIGH** 2 to 3 minutes or until slightly thickened. Stir occasionally. Add potatoes. Cook at **HIGH** 4 to 5 minutes; stir occasionally. Serve warm.

CINNAMON SWEET POTATOES

2 cans (16 oz. ea.) sweet potatoes or
  yams, drained
1/4 cup butter or margarine, melted
2 tablespoons packed brown sugar
2 eggs
Dash cinnamon or nutmeg
1/2 cup miniature marshmallows

Yield: 4 Servings

Combine potatoes, butter, sugar, eggs and cinnamon; mash until smooth. Spoon into 4 individual custard cups (10 oz. ea.). Cook at **HIGH** 5 to 6 minutes. Top with marshmallows. Cook 2 to 3 minutes, or until melted.

Eggs and Cheese

Main Dishes
SPECIAL HINTS FOR EGGS

Baked Eggs
- Use 6-ounce custard cup or coffee cup, generously greased, for each egg.
- Break egg into cup and with toothpick, pierce egg yolk twice and egg white several times.
- Top with one teaspoon milk.
- Cook, covered with plastic wrap, at **MEDIUM**.
- Let stand, covered, to complete cooking.

NUMBER OF EGGS	APPROXIMATE COOKING TIME (in minutes) at MEDIUM*	STAND TIME
1	$3/4$ to 1	1
2	$1^{1}/_4$ to $1^{1}/_2$	1
4	$2^{1}/_4$ to $2^{1}/_2$	$1^{1}/_2$

Poached Eggs
- Use 10-ounce custard cup or small glass bowl for each egg.
- Heat $1/4$ cup hot water, dash each vinegar and salt for each cup, at **HIGH**.
- Break egg into boiling water and with toothpick, pierce egg yolk twice and egg white several times.
- Cook, covered with plastic wrap, at **MEDIUM**.
- Let stand, covered, to complete cooking.

NUMBER OF EGGS	APPROXIMATE COOKING TIME (in minutes)		STAND TIME
	TO BOIL WATER at HIGH	TO POACH EGGS at MEDIUM*	
1	$1^{1}/_2$	$1/2$ to $3/4$	1
2	$2^{1}/_2$	$1^{1}/_2$ to $1^{3}/_4$	2
4	$3^{1}/_2$ to 4	$2^{1}/_4$ to $2^{1}/_2$	2

Scrambled Eggs
- Beat eggs and add 1 tablespoon milk and dash of salt for each egg.
- Pour into a greased glass container.
- Cook at **MEDIUM** according to time in the chart.
- Between first and second cooking time, stir eggs. Bring cooked portions along edge of dish to center.
- Stir and let stand.
- Eggs will continue to cook during stand and should be slightly underdone after cooking.

NUMBER OF EGGS	CONTAINER	APPROX. COOKING TIME (in minutes) at MEDIUM*		STAND TIME
		FIRST HEATING	SECOND HEATING	
1	1 cup glass measure	$1/2$ to $3/4$	$1/4$ to $1/2$	1
2	1 cup glass measure	$3/4$ to 1	$1/2$ to $3/4$	$1^{1}/_2$
4	1 qt. glass bowl	$1^{3}/_4$ to $2^{1}/_2$	1 to $1^{1}/_2$	$1^{1}/_2$
6	$1^{1}/_2$ qt. glass bowl	$2^{1}/_2$ to 3	1 to $1^{1}/_2$	2
8	$1^{1}/_2$ qt. glass bowl	3 to $3^{1}/_4$	2 to $2^{1}/_2$	2

*NOTE: Eggs will be slightly underdone after heating time. The cooking will be completed during stand time.

PREPARING HARD-COOKED EGGS

Cooking eggs in their shell is a microwave oven NO. Because you are unable to pierce the shell or the egg membrance, there is no place for the steam to escape. The result would be a messy egg, popping inside the oven.

HOWEVER, if the hard-cooked egg will be chopped, you can do this in the microwave oven. In greased small glass bowl, crack egg; with toothpick, pierce egg yolk twice and egg white several times. Cook, covered, at MEDIUM. Let stand to cool before chopping.

Pierce egg yolk and egg white before cooking.

NUMBER OF EGGS	APPROXIMATE COOKING TIME (in minutes) at MEDIUM
1	1 to 1½
2	2 to 2½
4	3½ to 4

BASIC OMELET

1 tablespoon butter or margarine
2 eggs
2 tablespoons milk
⅛ teaspoon salt
Dash pepper

Yield: 1 Serving
Cook butter in 9-inch glass pie plate at **LOW** 1 minute. Turn plate to coat bottom with butter. Meanwhile, combine remaining ingredients; pour into pie plate. Cover with plastic wrap. Cook at **MEDIUM** 2 to 2½ minutes, or until omelet is almost set; stir after 1 minute.
Let stand, covered, 2 minutes. With spatula, loosen edges of omelet from plate; fold into thirds to serve.

Variations:
For CHEESE omelet, *before folding, sprinkle* ¼ *cup shredded cheese down center of omelet.*

For HAM omelet, *before folding, sprinkle* ¼ *cup finely chopped cooked ham down center of omelet.*

For HERB omelet, *blend* ⅛ *teaspoon basil, thyme or crushed rosemary with eggs and milk.*

For JELLY omelet, *before folding, spoon* ¼ *cup jelly down center of omelet.*

NORMANDY OMELET

1 small apple, sliced
2 tablespoons butter or margarine, divided
1 tablespoon honey
Dash cinnamon
4 eggs, separated
Salt and pepper to taste

Yield: 2 Servings

In small glass bowl, combine apple, 1 tablespoon butter, honey and cinnamon. Cover with plastic wrap. Cook at **HIGH** 4 to 4½ minutes, or until apples are tender; reserve. Cook remaining butter in 9-inch glass pie plate at **HIGH** ½ to ¾ minute, or until melted; turn plate to coat bottom with butter. Meanwhile, beat egg whites until stiff, but not dry; beat egg yolks, salt and pepper until thickened. Fold egg yolks into egg whites; carefully pour mixture into pie plate. Cook at **MEDIUM** 4 to 5 minutes.
Let stand 2 minutes. With spatula, loosen edges of omelet from plate; spoon apples onto half. Fold other half omelet over apples; sprinkle, if desired, with confectioners sugar.

COUNTRY BREAKFAST

¼ cup butter or margarine
½ green pepper, chopped
1 small onion, chopped
2 cans (16 oz. ea.) sliced potatoes, drained
4 eggs
½ cup milk
½ teaspoon salt
⅛ teaspoon pepper
4 slices American cheese, halved, optional

Yield: 4 Servings

In 8-inch round dish, combine butter, green pepper and onion. Cook at **HIGH** 5 to 6 minutes, or until vegetables are tender; add potatoes. Combine eggs, milk, salt and pepper; stir into potatoes. Cover with plastic wrap. Cook at **MEDIUM** 9 to 10 minutes, or until eggs are set. Stir eggs every two minutes of cooking. Top with cheese; let stand, covered, 5 minutes before serving.

SIMPLE SATURDAY BREAKFAST

1 can (24 oz.) corned beef hash
2 tablespoons catsup
1 tablespoon Worcestershire sauce
½ teaspoon onion powder
⅛ teaspoon pepper
4 eggs

Yield: 4 Servings

In 8-inch round dish, combine hash, catsup, Worcestershire, onion powder and pepper. Cover with plastic wrap. Cook at **HIGH** 6 to 7 minutes; stir once. Lightly pat mixture into dish and form 4 wells. Into each well, break 1 egg; with toothpick, pierce egg yolk twice and egg white several times. Cook, covered, at **MEDIUM** 6 to 7 minutes, or until eggs are almost set. Let stand, covered, 5 minutes before serving.

SWISS SHRIMP FONDUE

1 can (10¾ oz.) condensed cream of shrimp soup
1 cup (4 oz.) shredded Swiss cheese
¼ cup white wine
½ teaspoon Worcestershire sauce
French bread, cut into 1-inch cubes or bread sticks

Yield: 4 Servings

In 1-quart casserole, combine soup, cheese, wine and Worcestershire sauce. Cook at **MEDIUM** 6 to 7 minutes, or until cheese is melted. Stir frequently. Serve hot with French bread.

WELSH RAREBIT

4 cups (1 pound) shredded Cheddar cheese
3 tablespoons flour
⅔ cup beer
½ teaspoon Worcestershire sauce
½ teaspoon dry mustard
Toast points

Yield: 4 Servings

Toss cheese with flour; set aside Place beer in 4-cup measure. Heat at **HIGH** 2 minutes, or until boiling.
Gradually stir in half of cheese, Worcestershire sauce and mustard; stir until smooth. Cook at **HIGH** 2 to 3 minutes.
Add remaining cheese and cook at **HIGH** 3 to 3½ minutes, or until cheese is completely melted; stir once. Serve over toast points.

MINI-PIZZA SNACKS

2 English muffins, split and toasted
¼ to ½ cup spaghetti sauce
½ cup (2 oz.) shredded mozzarella cheese
Oregano

Yield: 2 Servings

Arrange muffins on paper plate. Spread with spaghetti sauce. Top with cheese and sprinkle with oregano. Cook at **HIGH** 2 to 2½ minutes, or until cheese is melted.

Pasta, Grains and Cereals

Pastas

PREPARING PASTA TO COOK BY TIME

- Cover and heat hot water to a boil at **HIGH**.
- Add pasta and 1 teaspoon salt (¹/₂ tablespoon oil optional).
- Cook, uncovered at **HIGH**; stir once.
- Test pasta for desired doneness before adding more cooking time.

- Slightly undercook pasta that will be cooked again in casseroles.
- Stir and let stand, covered, 3 minutes.
- Drain and rinse before serving.

ITEM	CONTAINER	AMOUNT OF HOT WATER	APPROX. TIME TO BOIL WATER at HIGH (in minutes)	APPROX. TIME TO COOK PASTA at HIGH (in minutes)	STAND TIME (in minutes)
Egg Noodles medium width (8 oz.)	3-qt. casserole	1¹/₂ quart	13 to 15	9 to 10	3
Elbow Macaroni (8 oz.)	3-qt. casserole	1¹/₂ quart	13 to 15	11 to 13	3
Spaghetti (8 oz. broken)	3-qt. casserole	2 quarts	17 to 19	11 to 13	3

FETTUCCINE ALFREDO

1 package (8 oz.) medium egg noodles
1 cup grated Parmesan cheese
¹/₂ cup butter or margarine, cut into
   quarters
¹/₂ cup heavy cream
Pepper to taste

Yield: 4 Side-Dish Servings

Cook noodles according to chart above. While noodles are standing, in glass serving bowl, combine cheese, butter and cream. Cook at **MEDIUM** 4¹/₂ to 5¹/₂ minutes, or until butter is melted; stir twice.
Stir in drained noodles; toss well. Season with pepper.

BAKED ZITI

1 package (8 oz.) ziti macaroni, cooked
1 jar (15¹/₂ oz.) spaghetti sauce
¹/₂ cup (2 oz.) shredded mozzarella cheese

Yield: 4 Servings

Combine ziti and spaghetti sauce in 2-quart casserole. Cook, covered with glass lid, at **HIGH** 10 to 12 minutes; stir once. Sprinkle with cheese.
Let stand, covered, 10 minutes before serving.

FLORIDA-STYLE NOODLES

1 package (8 oz.) medium egg noodles
1/2 cup almonds
1/4 cup butter or margarine
1 tablespoon poppy seeds
1/2 tablespoon grated lemon peel
1/2 tablespoon grated orange peel
1/2 teaspoon salt
1/8 teaspoon pepper
1 cup sour cream

Yield: 4 Servings

Cook noodles according to chart, page 74. While noodles are standing, in glass serving bowl, cook almonds and butter at **HIGH** 2 to 3 minutes or until butter is melted. Stir in drained noodles, poppy seeds, lemon and orange peel, salt and pepper; toss well. Serve with sour cream.

SWISS NOODLE BAKE

4 slices bacon, diced
1 small onion, chopped
1 package (8 oz.) medium egg noodles, cooked (see page 74)
1 1/4 cups (5 oz.) shredded Swiss cheese
1 egg, beaten
2 tablespoons milk
1/2 teaspoon salt
1/4 teaspoon nutmeg
Pepper to taste
Buttered bread crumbs
1/8 teaspoon paprika

Yield: 6 Servings

Place bacon and onion in 2-quart casserole. Cook at **HIGH** 4 to 5 minutes or until bacon is crisp. Stir once. Drain. Stir in cooked noodles, cheese, egg, milk, salt, nutmeg and pepper. Cook, covered with glass lid, at **HIGH** 8 to 10 minutes or until heated through.
Let stand 5 minutes. Top with bread crumbs blended with paprika before serving.

MACARONI AND CHEESE

1 package (8 oz.) elbow macaroni, cooked and drained (see page 74)
3/4 pound pasteurized process cheese spread, cut into cubes
3/4 to 1 cup milk
1/2 to 3/4 teaspoon salt
1/4 teaspoon onion powder
1/4 teaspoon pepper
1/8 teaspoon dry mustard, optional
Buttered bread crumbs

Yield: 4 Servings

In 3-quart casserole, combine macaroni, cheese, milk, salt, onion, pepper and mustard. Cook, covered with glass lid, at **HIGH** 10 to 12 minutes; stir twice. Top with bread crumbs and cook, uncovered, at **HIGH** 3 to 5 minutes.

NOODLE PUDDING

1 package (8 oz.) medium egg noodles
1/2 cup butter or margarine
4 eggs, beaten
1 cup cottage cheese
1 cup sour cream
3/4 cup raisins
1/2 cup sugar
1 teaspoon cinnamon
1/4 teaspoon nutmeg

Yield: 8 Servings

Cook noodles according to chart, page 74. In 2-quart casserole, cook butter at **MEDIUM** 2 1/2 minutes, or until melted. In large bowl, combine butter, remaining ingredients and drained noodles; pour into same casserole. Sprinkle, if desired, with additional cinnamon. Cook at **MEDIUM** 18 to 20 minutes until pudding is set. Let stand, covered with lid, 5 minutes. Serve warm or chilled.

Rice and Other Grains

PREPARING RICE AND OTHER GRAINS

- Cover and heat hot water to a boil at **HIGH**.

- Add grain, salt and butter (amount of salt and butter as package directs).

- Cook, covered, at **MEDIUM**.

- Let stand, covered, before serving.

*Note: **For instant (no cook) products,** using package directions, bring hot water to a boil. (See Heating Liquids chart page 28). Stir in product; let stand, covered.*

ITEM	CONTAINER	AMOUNT OF HOT WATER	APPROX. TIME TO BOIL WATER at HIGH (in minutes)	APPROX. TIME TO COOK GRAIN at MEDIUM (in minutes)	STAND TIME (in minutes)
RICE					
Brown (1 cup)	2-qt. casserole	3 cups	7 to 8	40 to 45 →	25
Flavored Rice Mix (6 oz.)	2-qt. casserole	as package directs	6 to 7	20 →	10
Long Grain (1 cup)	2-qt. casserole	2 cups	6 to 7	11 to 13 →	10
Long Grain & Wild Rice Mix (6 oz.)	2-qt. casserole	2½ cups	7 to 8	20 to 22 →	5
Quick Rice (1 cup)	1-qt. casserole	1 cup	4 to 5	4 →	5
Short Grain (1 cup)	2-qt. casserole	2 cups	6 to 7	9 to 10 →	10
BARLEY					
Quick Cook (1 cup)	2-qt. casserole	3 cups	7 to 8	8 to 10 →	3 (then drain)
GRITS (⅔ cup)	3-qt casserole	3⅓ cups	8 to 9	10 →	10

BARLEY MUSHROOM CASSEROLE

6 tablespoons butter or margarine
2 medium onions, finely chopped
3 cloves garlic, finely chopped
1 pound fresh mushrooms, sliced
1 cup quick cooking barley
3/4 cup chicken broth
1/4 cup chopped parsley
2 teaspoons basil
1 teaspoon salt
1/4 teaspoon pepper

Yield: 6 Servings

In 2 1/2-quart casserole, combine butter, onion and garlic. Cook, covered with glass lid, at **HIGH** 4 to 5 minutes or until onion is tender. Stir in remaining ingredients. Cook, covered, at **HIGH** 7 minutes and at **MEDIUM** 12 to 14 minutes or until barley is tender.
Let stand, covered, 5 minutes before serving.

SPANISH RICE

1 medium onion, chopped
1/4 cup finely chopped green pepper
2 tablespoons butter or margarine
Water
1 can (16 oz.) stewed tomatoes, drained and chopped; reserve liquid
1 cup long grain rice
1 1/2 teaspoons salt
1/8 teaspoon pepper

Yield: 6 Servings

In 2-quart casserole, combine onion, green pepper and butter. Cook at **HIGH** 4 to 5 minutes; stir once. Add enough water to reserved liquid to equal 2 cups. Add to dish with tomatoes, rice, salt and pepper. Cook, covered with glass lid, at **HIGH** 8 to 9 minutes and at **MEDIUM** 15 to 17 minutes or until rice is tender; stir once.
Let stand, covered, 5 minutes before serving.

HOPPIN' JOHN

4 slices bacon, diced
1 medium onion, chopped
2 1/2 cups hot water
1 1/2 cups cooked black-eyed peas
1 cup long grain rice
1 teaspoon salt
1/4 teaspoon pepper
Dash hot pepper sauce, optional

Yield: 6 Servings

Place bacon and onion in 3-quart casserole. Cook at **HIGH** 7 to 9 minutes or until bacon is crisp. Stir once. Stir in remaining ingredients. Cook, covered with glass lid, at **HIGH** 7 to 8 minutes, or until liquid boils. Cook, covered at **MEDIUM** 14 to 16 minutes or until rice is tender; stir twice.
Let stand, covered, 10 minutes before serving.

GRANOLA CEREAL

2 cups quick or old fashioned oats
2/3 cup soy nuts or finely chopped nuts
1/3 cup wheat germ, optional
1/4 cup packed brown sugar
1/3 cup coconut or raisins
1/4 cup honey
1 teaspoon vanilla

Yield: 4 Cups

Place oats in 8-inch dish. Cook at **HIGH** 5 to 6 minutes; stir twice. Add soy nuts, wheat germ, brown sugar and coconut; stir in honey and vanilla. Cook at **HIGH** 6 to 7 minutes; stir twice. Cool completely; stir occasionally to crumble.

Cereals

PREPARING HOT CEREALS

- Combine cereal, hot water* and salt (optional) in bowl or individual dish.

- Cook, stirring twice.

- Let stand; stir before serving.

- Top as desired, with sugar, spices, etc.

For Cream of Wheat and Farina, heat water to a boil, then add cereal.

ITEM	CONTAINER	AMOUNT OF HOT WATER	AMOUNT OF CEREAL	APPROX. COOKING TIME (in minutes)		STAND TIME (in minutes)
				at HIGH	at LOW	
Cream of Wheat (Regular)						
1 serving	1-qt. glass bowl	1¼ cups	2½ tablespoons	—	2 to 3 →	1
2 servings	1½-qt. glass bowl	2 cups	⅓ cup	—	4 to 5 →	1
Farina						
1 serving	1-qt. glass bowl	1 cup	3 tablespoons	—	2 to 3 →	1
2 servings	1½-qt. glass bowl	2 cups	6 tablespoons	—	4 to 5 →	1
Oatmeal (Quick)						
1 serving	individual serving dish	¾ cup	⅓ cup	1 to 1½	— →	1
2 servings	2 individual serving dishes	1½ cups	⅔ cup	2 to 2½	— →	1
4 servings	1-qt. glass bowl	3 cups	1⅓ cups	3½ to 4	— →	2
Wheat-Bran Cereal						
1 serving	individual serving dish	¾ cup	¼ cup	3	— →	1
2 servings	2 individual serving dishes	1½ cups	½ cup	5 to 6	— →	1
4 servings	2-qt. glass bowl	3 cups	1 cup	7 to 6	— →	2

Quick Breads

DIRECTIONS FOR BAKING QUICK BREADS, MUFFINS AND COFFEE CAKES

- Prepare batter according to package or recipe directions.
- Use dishes recommended in chart or recipes. Glass dishes allow the bottom of the cakes or breads to be checked for doneness. When the product is removed from the oven, visually check bottom.
- Grease the bottom of the dish when coffee cakes are to be directly served from the dish.
- Grease bottom and sides of the dish and line the bottom of the dish with wax paper when the product is to be inverted and removed from the dish.
- Never flour the dish.
- Loaf dishes may be shielded on each end with a 3-inch wide strip of foil, if necessary. Mold foil around dish. Remove foil during the last 1 to $1\frac{1}{2}$ minutes of cooking.
- Square dishes may be shielded on each corner with a triangle of foil, if necessary. Mold foil around dish. Remove foil during last 1 to $1\frac{1}{2}$ minutes of cooking.
- When cooking muffins, line microwave muffin pans with paper baking cups. Fill paper baking cups $\frac{2}{3}$ full.
- Most package mixes and some recipes benefit from 2-stage cooking. We have given 2-stage cooking directions where they are helpful.
- Check quick breads and coffee cakes during cooking. Different brands vary in ingredients and density of batter; cooking times may be slightly different than those given in chart.
- After cooking, test for doneness. Top of product may be sticky to the touch, but should not have any uncooked batter. A toothpick inserted near center should come out clean.
- Let stand, uncovered, on a flat surface for 10 to 15 minutes. Stand time is important to allow product to finish baking.
- Cakes and breads that are to be inverted should be loosened from the sides of the dish. Carefully turn product out of dish and peel off wax paper.
- Store, covered, until ready to serve.

QUICK BREAD MIX CHART

ITEM	AMOUNT OF BATTER	DISH SIZE/ PREPARATION	FIRST STAGE	→	SECOND STAGE	SPECIAL INSTRUCTIONS	STAND TIME
Coffee Cake Crumb Topping (10.5 oz.)	All batter	Grease 8 or 9-inch round or square dish.	LOW 6 minutes	→	HIGH 3 to $3\frac{1}{2}$ minutes	—	10 minutes, uncovered
Quick Bread ($14\frac{1}{2}$ to 17 oz.)	All batter	Grease 9×5×3-inch loaf dish. Line bottom with wax paper.	LOW 10 minutes	→	HIGH $3\frac{1}{2}$ to 4 minutes	Cover with wax paper.	15 minutes, uncovered
Corn Bread (10 to 12 oz.)	All batter	Grease 8 or 9-inch round or square dish.	LOW 6 minutes	→	HIGH $2\frac{1}{2}$ to $3\frac{1}{2}$ minutes	Increase milk by 2 Tbsp. Add 1 Tbsp. oil to batter.	10 minutes, uncovered
Gingerbread (14 oz.)	All batter	Grease 8-inch square dish.	MEDIUM $9\frac{1}{2}$ to $10\frac{1}{2}$ minutes		—	—	15 minutes, uncovered
Muffins (cook 6 at a time)	Scant $\frac{1}{4}$ cup per muffin	6-cup muffin pan lined with paper baking cups.	MEDIUM $4\frac{1}{2}$ to $5\frac{1}{2}$ minutes		—	—	5 minutes, uncovered

IRISH SODA BREAD

2¾ cups flour
3 tablespoons sugar
¾ teaspoon salt
¾ teaspoon baking powder
4 tablespoons butter or margarine
1½ cups raisins
1 tablespoon caraway seeds
1 cup buttermilk
1 egg
¾ teaspoon baking soda

Yield: 6 Servings

Sift together flour, sugar, salt and baking powder; cut in butter. Stir in raisins and caraway. Combine buttermilk, egg and baking soda; add to dry ingredients. Stir only until flour is moistened. On floured board, lightly knead dough until smooth, about 3 minutes. Shape into ball and place in 1½-quart glass bowl, bottom lined with wax paper; cut an "X" across top of dough. Cover with wax paper. Cook at **MEDIUM** 8 to 10 minutes.
Let stand, uncovered, 10 minutes; turn out of bowl. Let stand upside-down an additional 10 minutes; store, covered, until ready to serve.

BASIC NUT BREAD

½ cup packed brown sugar
3 tablespoons butter or margarine
2 eggs
¾ cup buttermilk
½ teaspoon vanilla
1¼ cups flour
¾ cup chopped nuts
1½ teaspoons baking powder
1 teaspoon cinnamon
½ teaspoon salt
Cinnamon sugar

Yield: 1 Loaf

Cream together sugar and butter. Stir in eggs, buttermilk and vanilla. Add flour, nuts, baking powder, cinnamon and salt; stir only until flour is moistened. Spoon batter into greased 9"×5"×3" glass loaf dish, bottom lined with wax paper. Sprinkle with cinnamon sugar. Cover with wax paper. Cook at **MEDIUM** 8 to 9 minutes or until toothpick inserted near center comes out clean.
Let stand 15 minutes. Invert and remove wax paper; let stand 5 minutes. Store, covered, until ready to serve.

BOSTON BROWN BREAD

1 cup buttermilk
½ cup molasses
½ cup raisins
½ teaspoon baking powder
½ teaspoon baking soda
½ teaspoon salt
½ cup whole wheat flour
½ cup yellow cornmeal
¼ cup flour

Yield: 1 Loaf

Combine buttermilk and molasses; stir in raisins, baking powder, baking soda and salt. Add flours and cornmeal; stir only until moistened. Pour batter into generously greased 4-cup glass measure. Cover loosely with plastic wrap; secure wrap with rubber band. Rubber band should be secured under the handle of glass measure. Cook at **MEDIUM** 8 to 10 minutes.
Let stand, uncovered, 10 minutes. Remove from dish; let stand 5 minutes. Store, covered, until ready to serve.

CHERRY BRUNCH ROLLS

½ cup packed brown sugar
¼ cup chopped maraschino cherries
¼ cup flaked coconut
1 tablespoon water
¼ teaspoon cinnamon
1 can (8 oz.) refrigerated biscuits
3 tablespoons butter or margarine, melted

Yield: 10 Rolls

In small glass bowl, combine brown sugar, cherries, coconut, water and cinnamon. Stir until smooth. Cook at **HIGH** 2 to 2½ minutes. Pour into a greased 5-cup ring mold. Dip each biscuit into melted butter. Arrange biscuits on top of cherry mixture. Cook at **MEDIUM** 4 to 4½ minutes. Let stand, covered, 5 minutes before inverting on serving platter. Store, covered, until ready to serve.

SIESTA CORNBREAD

1 package (12 oz.) corn muffin mix
1 medium onion, chopped
2 tablespoons chopped pimiento
1 to 2 tablespoons chopped jalapeno
 peppers
1 can (8¼ oz.) cream-style corn
1 egg
¼ cup milk
2 tablespoons oil

Yield: 6 Servings

Combine corn muffin mix, onion, pimento and peppers; stir in corn, egg, milk and oil. Spoon batter into greased 2-quart ring mold. Cook at **MEDIUM** 12 to 14 minutes, or until bread pulls away from center and sides of dish.
Let stand 10 minutes. Invert from dish and serve warm.

SOUTHERN CHEESE SPOON BREAD

½ cup yellow cornmeal
2 cups milk
¾ teaspoon salt
2 eggs, beaten
1 cup (4 oz.) diced American cheese
2 tablespoons butter or margarine

Yield: 6 Servings

In medium glass bowl, combine cornmeal, milk and salt. Cook at **HIGH** 3 minutes and at **MEDIUM** 4 to 5 minutes or until cornmeal is thickened; stir twice. Stir until smooth; add eggs, cheese and butter. Stir until cheese and butter are almost melted. Pour into greased 1-quart casserole. Cook, covered with glass lid, at **MEDIUM** 5 to 7 minutes, or until center is almost set.
Let stand 10 minutes before serving.

RAISIN BRAN MUFFINS

2½ cups bran flakes cereal
1 cup milk
1¼ cups flour
½ to ¾ cup raisins
⅓ cup sugar
1 tablespoon baking powder
½ teaspoon salt
¼ teaspoon cinnamon
1 egg
¼ cup oil

Yield: 12 Muffins

Combine bran flakes and milk in large bowl. Stir until flakes are moistened; let stand 2 to 3 minutes.
Meanwhile, combine flour, raisins, sugar, baking powder, salt and cinnamon. Into cereal mixture, stir in egg and oil; add flour mixture, stirring only until flour is moistened. Line 6-cup muffin pan with paper baking cups; fill ⅔ full. Cook at **MEDIUM** 4 to 5 minutes; repeat procedure with remaining batter.
Let stand 5 minutes; store, covered, until ready to serve.

PUMPKIN PECAN MUFFINS

⅔ cup sugar
½ cup cooked pumpkin
1 egg
½ cup chopped pecans or walnuts
½ cup raisins
¼ cup milk
3 tablespoons oil
1 to 1¼ teaspoons pumpkin pie spice
⅛ teaspoon salt
1 cup flour
1 teaspoon baking powder

Yield: 9 Muffins

Combine sugar, pumpkin, egg, pecans, raisins, milk, oil, pumpkin pie spice and salt; add flour and baking powder. Stir only until flour is moistened. Line 6-cup muffin pan with paper baking cups; fill ⅔ full. Cook at **MEDIUM** 5 to 6 minutes; repeat procedure with remaining batter, filling 3 cups. Cook at **MEDIUM** 3 to 4 minutes.
Let stand 5 minutes; store, covered, until ready to serve.

SUGARY JAM MUFFINS

¼ cup shortening
¼ cup sugar
1 egg
¼ cup milk
1 cup flour
¾ teaspoon baking powder
¼ teaspoon salt
2 tablespoons jam
2 tablespoons butter or margarine
2 tablespoons cinnamon sugar

Yield: 6 Muffins

Cream together shortening and sugar; stir in egg and milk. Add flour, baking powder and salt; stir only until flour is moistened. Line 6-cup muffin pan with paper baking cups. Divide half of batter into 6 cups. Spoon 1 teaspoon of jam into center of each. Top with remaining batter, spreading to cover jam. Cook at **MEDIUM** 4½ to 5 minutes.
Let stand, covered, 3 minutes.
Meanwhile, cook butter at **MEDIUM** ½ to ¾ minute or until melted. Dip tops of muffins in butter, then in cinnamon sugar. Store, covered, until ready to serve.

PEACHY MUFFINS

1 can (8 oz.) sliced peaches, drained; reserve ¼ cup syrup
⅓ packed brown sugar
3 tablespoons butter or margarine
1 egg
1 cup flour
½ cup chopped pecans
1 teaspoon baking powder
½ teaspoon salt

Yield: 9 Muffins

Finely chop ¼ cup peaches; set aside. Cream together remaining peaches, sugar and butter; stir in egg and reserved syrup. Add flour, pecans, baking powder and salt; stir only until flour is moistened. Stir in chopped peaches. Line 6-cup muffin pan with paper baking cups; fill ⅔ full. Cook at **MEDIUM** 5 to 6 minutes; repeat procedure with remaining batter, filling 3 cups. Cook at **MEDIUM** 2 to 3 minutes.
Let stand 5 minutes; store, covered, until ready to serve.

EASY MORNING MUFFINS

½ cup milk
½ cup oil
2 eggs
½ cup sugar
2 cups flour
1 tablespoon baking powder
½ teaspoon salt

Yield: 12 Muffins

Combine milk, oil, eggs and sugar; add remaining ingredients. Stir only until flour is moistened. Line 6-cup muffin pan with paper baking cups; fill ⅔ full. Cook at **MEDIUM** 3 to 4 minutes; repeat procedure with remaining batter.
Let stand 5 minutes. If desired, dip tops of muffins in melted butter, then in cinnamon sugar. Store, covered, until ready to serve.

BANANA NUT COFFEE CAKE

¼ cup oil
¼ cup milk
1 egg
1 mashed ripe banana
½ cup packed brown sugar
¾ cup flour
½ cup chopped nuts
¾ teaspoon baking powder
¼ teaspoon salt
¼ teaspoon baking soda

Nut Topping:
¼ cup packed brown sugar
¼ cup chopped nuts
2 tablespoons flour
⅛ teaspoon cinnamon
1 tablespoon butter or margarine, softened

Yield: 8 Servings

In medium bowl, combine oil, milk, egg, banana and sugar. Add flour, nuts, baking powder, salt and baking soda; stir only until flour is moistened. Pour into greased 8 or 9-inch round dish.
In small bowl, prepare Nut Topping. Combine brown sugar, nuts, flour, and cinnamon; cut in butter. Sprinkle over batter. Cook at **MEDIUM** 9 to 10 minutes, or until toothpick inserted near center comes out clean.
Let stand 10 minutes. Store, covered, until ready to serve.

HOLIDAY CRANBERRY COFFEE CAKE

1 can (8 oz.) whole berry cranberry sauce
6 tablespoons sugar, divided
1/4 cup chopped nuts, optional
1 tablespoon butter or margarine, melted
2 cups buttermilk biscuit mix
1 cup orange juice or apple juice
1 egg

Glaze:
1 cup confectioners sugar
1 to 2 tablespoons water
1/2 teaspoon vanilla

Yield: 8 Servings

In small bowl, combine cranberry sauce, 4 tablespoons sugar, nuts and butter. Cook at **HIGH** 2 to 2 1/2 minutes. Spread into 8-inch round dish, bottom lined with wax paper. Combine biscuit mix, juice, egg and remaining sugar, blending until smooth. Spoon batter over cranberry mixture. Cover with wax paper. Cook at **LOW** 8 minutes and at **HIGH** 4 to 6 minutes, or until toothpick inserted near center comes out clean.
Let stand, uncovered, 10 minutes before inverting onto platter; carefully peel off wax paper. Store, covered, until ready to serve. Meanwhile, combine sugar, water and vanilla. Stir until smooth. Drizzle over cake just before serving.

MARMALADE GINGERBREAD

1 package (14 oz.) gingerbread mix
3/4 cup orange juice
1/2 cup orange marmalade

Yield: 8 Servings

Combine gingerbread mix, orange juice and marmalade; blend according to package directions. Pour into greased 8 or 9-inch square dish. Cook at **LOW** 8 minutes and at **HIGH** 6 1/2 to 7 1/2 minutes, or until toothpick inserted near center comes out clean.
Let stand 10 minutes. Store, covered, until ready to serve.

GRAHAM STREUSEL COFFEE CAKE

1/2 cup butter or margarine, melted
1 cup graham cracker crumbs
1/2 cup packed brown sugar
1/3 cup chopped nuts
3/4 teaspoon cinnamon
1 package (18 1/2 oz.) yellow cake mix
4 eggs
1 cup water
1/3 cup oil

Vanilla Glaze:
2 cups confectioners sugar
2 to 3 tablespoons water
1 teaspoon vanilla

Yield: 10 Servings

In medium bowl, combine butter, crumbs, sugar, nuts and cinnamon. Divide crumb mixture into two 8-inch round dishes, bottoms lined with wax paper. Spread to cover bottom of dishes. In large bowl, with electric mixer, blend cake mix, eggs, water and oil at low speed 1/2 minute; beat at medium speed 3 minutes. Pour about 2 cups batter into each dish. Cover with wax paper. Cook at **LOW** 6 minutes and at **HIGH** 4 to 5 minutes, or until toothpick inserted near center comes out clean. Let stand, uncovered, 10 minutes. Repeat procedure with remaining dish.
Prepare Vanilla Glaze in medium bowl. Combine sugar, water and vanilla; stir well.
With knife, loosen cake from sides of dish. Invert one cake onto serving platter; carefully peel off wax paper. Invert second layer onto paper plate; carefully peel off wax paper. Cover until cool. Just before serving, spread half of glaze on cake on serving platter; top with second layer. Drizzle with remaining glaze.

Desserts and Candy

DIRECTIONS FOR CAKES AND CUPCAKES

- Layer cakes must be baked one layer at a time. Or, the entire cake mix may be baked in a 16 cup fluted tube dish.

- Prepare batter according to package or recipe directions.

- Use dishes recommended in chart or recipes. Glass dishes allow the bottom of the cakes to be checked for doneness. When the product is removed from the oven, visually check bottom.

- Grease the bottom of the dish when cakes are to be served directly from the dish.

- Grease the bottom and sides of dish when cake is to be inverted and removed from dish, such as layer cakes, upside-down cakes. If desired, bottom of dish may be lined with wax paper.

- Use only 2 to 2$^1/_4$ cups of batter for an 8 or 9-inch round or square dish. Cook second layer immediately after the first. The remaining batter can be used for cupcakes.

- When using fluted tube dish, be sure to grease sides and "tube." All the batter from a 2 layer cake mix may be poured into a 16 cup fluted tube dish.

- Never flour cake dishes, fluted tube dishes or muffin pans.

- Square dishes may be shielded on each corner with a triangle of foil, if necessary. Mold foil around dish. Remove foil during last 1 to 1$^1/_2$ minutes of cooking.

- When cooking cupcakes, line microwave muffin pans with paper baking cups. Fill paper baking cups half full.

- Cover with wax paper when indicated in chart or recipe.

- Most package mixes and some recipes benefit from 2-stage cooking. We have given 2-stage cooking directions where they are helpful.

- Check cakes during cooking. Different brands vary in ingredients and density of batter; cooking times may be slightly different than those given in chart.

- After cooking, test for doneness. Top of cakes or cupcakes may be sticky to the touch but should not have any uncooked batter. The cake should have slightly pulled away from the edge of the dish. A toothpick inserted near the center should come out clean.

- Let stand, uncovered on a flat surface for 5 to 15 minutes. Stand time is important to allow cakes and cupcakes to finish baking.

- Cakes that are to be inverted should be loosened from the sides of the dish. Carefully turn cake out of dish.

- Store, covered, until ready to serve.

- Frost, if desired, when completely cooled. Microwave cakes are very tender and may tear, if too much pressure is applied when they are frosted.

CAKE MIX CHART

ITEM	AMOUNT OF BATTER	DISH SIZE/ PREPARATION	FIRST STAGE →	SECOND STAGE	SPECIAL INSTRUC- TIONS	STAND TIME
Cake Mix (18³/₄ to 20¹/₄ oz.)	2¹/₄ cups	Grease 8 or 9-inch round or square dish.	LOW 6 minutes	HIGH 3¹/₂ to 4¹/₂ minutes	Cover with wax paper.	10 minutes, uncovered
Cake Mix (18³/₄ to 20¹/₄ oz.)	All batter	Grease 16-cup fluted tube dish.	LOW 10 minutes	HIGH 6¹/₂ to 7 minutes	Cover dish with wax paper during last minute of cooking.	15 minutes, uncovered
Brownies (15 oz.) Cake-Like	All batter	8 or 9-inch round or square dish.	MEDIUM 8¹/₂ to 9¹/₂ minutes	—	—	until completely cool
Cupcakes	2 rounded tablespoons per cup- cake	Muffin pan lined with paper baking cups 1 2 4 6	MEDIUM 45 sec. to 1 min. 1 to 1¹/₄ minutes 2¹/₂ to 3¹/₄ minutes 4¹/₂ to 5 minutes	—	—	5 minutes, uncovered
Mix-in-Dish Cake No frosting	All batter	Grease 8 or 9-inch round or square dish.	LOW 8 minutes	HIGH 3¹/₂ to 4¹/₂ minutes	Cover dish with wax paper last minute of cooking.	10 minutes, uncovered
Mix-in-Dish Cake With frosting	All batter	Cardboard pan provided with mix.	LOW 5 minutes	HIGH 2¹/₂ to 3 minutes	—	until cool, uncovered

APPLESAUCE CAKE

2 cups flour
1 cup chopped walnuts
1 tablespoon cinnamon
2 teaspoons baking soda
1½ teaspoons salt
1 teaspoon baking powder
1 teaspoon nutmeg
¼ teaspoon cloves
1½ cups sugar
½ cup oil
3 eggs
1 jar (15 oz.) applesauce

Yield: 12 Servings

Mix flour, walnuts, cinnamon, baking soda, salt, baking powder, nutmeg and cloves; set aside. In mixer bowl, beat sugar, oil and eggs at high speed for 5 minutes. Alternately blend in flour mixture and applesauce; beat until smooth. Pour batter into well greased 16-cup fluted tube dish. Cover with wax paper. Cook at **LOW** for 10 minutes and at **HIGH** 9 to 10 minutes, or until toothpick inserted in center comes out clean. Let stand 15 minutes, uncovered, then invert onto serving plate.

YELLOW CAKE

¾ cup sugar
⅓ cup butter or margarine, softened
1 egg
⅔ cup milk
1 teaspoon vanilla
1 cup flour
1½ teaspoons baking powder
¼ teaspoon salt

Yield: 1 Layer

Cream sugar and butter in large bowl with electric mixer. Add egg; beat well. Stir in remaining ingredients. Beat 1 minute at medium speed. Grease an 8 or 9-inch round dish. Pour batter into dish; cover with wax paper. Cook at **LOW** for 6 minutes and at **HIGH** 5 to 6 minutes, or until toothpick inserted near center comes out clean.
Let stand, uncovered, 15 minutes. Invert onto serving dish. Store covered.

PINEAPPLE UPSIDE-DOWN CAKE

6 tablespoons butter or margarine
1 cup packed brown sugar
2 tablespoons water
1 can (20 oz.) sliced pineapple, drained; reserve syrup
10 maraschino cherries
1 package (18½ oz.) yellow cake mix
Ingredients as cake package directs

Yield: 2 Layers

In small glass bowl, cook butter, brown sugar and water at **HIGH** 3 to 4 minutes, or until mixture boils 1 minute. In two 8 or 9-inch round dishes, spread sugar-butter mixture; arrange pineapple and cherries. Prepare cake mix according to package directions using reserved syrup as part of water. Pour 2¼ cups of batter into each dish. Cover with wax paper. Cook at **LOW** 6 minutes and at **HIGH** 5 to 6 minutes, or until toothpick inserted near center comes out clean.
Let stand, 10 minutes.
Repeat with remaining layer. With knife loosen cake from sides of dish; invert onto serving platter. Store covered.

CARROT SPICE CAKE   *7-20-08*

Great

1¼ cups flour
1 cup packed brown sugar
1 teaspoon baking powder
1 teaspoon baking soda
2 teaspoons cinnamon
½ teaspoon allspice
½ teaspoon salt
1¼ cups shredded carrot
⅔ cup oil
2 eggs
1 can (8 oz.) crushed pineapple, drained
1 teaspoon vanilla
½ cup chopped nuts
¼ cup raisins

Yield: 8 Servings

In large bowl, with electric mixer, combine flour, sugar, baking powder, baking soda, cinnamon, allspice, salt and carrot. Stir in oil, eggs, pineapple and vanilla and beat 2 minutes at medium speed. Stir in nuts and raisins. Pour batter into a greased 10 to 12-cup fluted tube dish. Cover with wax paper. Cook at **MEDIUM** 11½ to 12½ minutes, or until toothpick inserted near center comes out clean.
Let stand, uncovered, 10 minutes. Store, covered, until ready to serve.

CIDER SPICE CAKE

2¼ cups flour
2 teaspoons cinnamon
1 teaspoon nutmeg
1 teaspoon salt
1 teaspoon baking soda
½ teaspoon cloves
1½ cups sugar
½ cup butter or margarine, softened
1 egg
1¼ cups apple cider or juice
1 cup raisins
2 tablespoons flour
Confectioners sugar

Yield: 12 Servings

Combine 2¼ cups flour, cinnamon, nutmeg, salt, baking soda and cloves. Cream sugar and butter with electric mixer; add egg. Alternately add flour mixture and cider, mixing until smooth; fold in raisins tossed with 2 tablespoons flour. Pour batter into greased 16-cup fluted tube dish. Cover with wax paper. Cook at **LOW** 10 minutes and at **HIGH** 5 to 6 minutes, or until toothpick inserted near center comes out clean. Let stand, uncovered, 15 minutes, before inverting onto serving platter. Let stand until cool. Just before serving, sprinkle with confectioners sugar.

GERMAN CHOCOLATE UPSIDE-DOWN CAKE

½ cup packed brown sugar
⅓ cup butter or margarine
Pecan halves
½ cup flaked coconut
2 tablespoons milk
Single layer chocolate cake mix
Ingredients as cake package directs

Yield: 8 Servings

Place sugar and butter in small glass bowl. Cook at **LOW** 1½ to 2 minutes, or until butter is melted. Stir until smooth. Spread butter mixture into greased and lined 8 or 9-inch round dish. Arrange pecans on top. Sprinkle with coconut and drizzle with milk. Prepare cake mix according to package directions; pour over coconut. Cover with wax paper. Cook at **LOW** 6 minutes and at **HIGH** 2½ to 3½ minutes, or until toothpick inserted near center comes out clean.
Let stand, uncovered, 10 minutes. Invert onto serving platter; carefully peel off wax paper. Store, covered, until cool.

CHOCOLATE SPICE CAKE

1 cup flour
1 cup packed brown sugar
¼ cup cocoa
1 teaspoon baking soda
¾ teaspoon allspice
½ teaspoon salt
½ teaspoon cinnamon
½ teaspoon ginger
1 cup water
¼ cup vegetable oil
2 tablespoons white vinegar
1 teaspoon vanilla

Yield: 8 Servings

In 8-inch round dish, combine flour, sugar, cocoa, baking soda, allspice, salt, cinnamon and ginger. Combine water, oil, vinegar and vanilla; pour into flour mixture. Mix with fork until well blended. Cook at **MEDIUM** 14 to 15 minutes, or until toothpick inserted near center comes out clean.
Let stand to cool. Store covered.

DEVIL'S FOOD CAKE

¾ cup sugar
⅓ cup shortening
1 egg
⅔ cup hot water
¾ cup flour
¼ cup unsweetened cocoa
½ teaspoon baking soda
½ teaspoon salt
½ teaspoon vanilla
¼ teaspoon baking powder

Yield: 1 Layer

Cream sugar and shortening with electric mixer. Add egg and water. Stir in remaining ingredients and blend until smooth. Pour batter into greased 8 or 9-inch round dish, bottom lined with wax paper. Cook at **LOW** 6 minutes and at **HIGH** 3½ to 4½ minutes, or until toothpick inserted near center comes out clean.
Let stand 10 minutes, then invent onto serving plate. Store covered.

CHOCOLATE POUND CAKE

1 package (18½ oz.) chocolate cake mix
1 package (4½ oz.) instant chocolate
  pudding mix
4 eggs
1 cup water
¼ cup oil

Yield: 12 Servings

Combine all ingredients in large bowl. Beat at medium speed with electric mixer 4 minutes. Pour batter into greased 16-cup fluted tube dish. Cover with wax paper. Cook at **LOW** 10 minutes and at **HIGH** 6 to 7 minutes, or until toothpick inserted near center comes out clean. Let stand, uncovered , 15 minutes before inverting onto serving platter. Let stand, covered, until cool.

PLANTATION COCONUT CAKE

1 package (18½ oz.) yellow cake mix
1 package (3¾ oz.) instant coconut cream
  or instant vanilla pudding mix
4 eggs
1 cup water
⅓ cup oil
1 jar (12 oz.) strawberry or raspberry
  preserves

Creamy Glaze:
1½ cups confectioners sugar
2 to 2½ tablespoons milk
2 tablespoons butter or margarine,
  softened
2 drops red food colorings, optional
Flaked coconut

Yield: 12 Servings

In a large bowl with electric mixer, combine cake mix, pudding mix, eggs, water and oil; beat at medium speed 2 minutes. Pour batter into greased 16-cup fluted tube dish. Cover with wax paper. Cook at **LOW** 10 minutes and at **HIGH** 6 to 7 minutes, or until toothpick inserted near center comes out clean.
Let stand, uncovered, 15 minutes before inverting on platter. Let stand, covered, until cool.
Split cake into 3 layers; spread in between with preserves. Prepare glaze in small bowl. Combine sugar, milk, and butter; stir until smooth. Drizzle over cake; sprinkle with coconut. Store, covered.

FESTIVE RUM CAKE

1 cup finely chopped pecans or walnuts
1 package (18½ oz.) yellow cake mix
1 package (3¾ oz.) instant vanilla pudding
  mix
4 eggs
½ cup water
½ cup oil
½ cup dark rum

Rum Glaze:
1 cup sugar
½ cup butter or margarine, melted
¼ cup water
¼ to ⅓ cup dark rum

Yield: 12 Servings

Sprinkle nuts in generously greased 16-cup fluted tube dish. In large bowl, with electric mixer, combine cake mix, pudding mix, eggs, water, oil and rum; beat at medium speed 4 minutes. Pour batter evenly over nuts. Cover with wax paper. Cook at **LOW** 10 minutes and at **HIGH** 5 to 6 minutes, or until toothpick inserted near center comes out clean. Let stand, uncovered, 15 minutes. In 2-cup measure combine sugar, butter, and water; mix well. Cook at **HIGH** 2 to 2½ minutes, or until boiling; stir in rum. Prick top of cake; drizzle half of Rum Glaze over cake (to absorb). Invert cake onto serving platter and prick top and sides of cake; drizzle cake with remaining glaze. Store, covered, until ready to serve.

CREAMY CHEESECAKE

1 package (8 oz.) cream cheese, softened
½ cup sugar
1 egg
1 teaspoon vanilla
1 cup sour cream
9-inch graham cracker crumb crust, baked
  (see page 97)

Yield: 8 Servings

In medium bowl, combine cream cheese, sugar, egg, and vanilla until smooth; stir in sour cream. Cook at **MEDIUM** 3 to 5 minutes; stir twice. Pour cheese mixture into pie crust. Cook at **MEDIUM** 3 to 4 minutes, or until center is almost set. Chill at least 3 hours or overnight.

TOFFEE FONDUE

1 package (14 oz.) caramels
1/4 cup strong coffee
2 to 4 tablespoons milk
1/2 cup milk chocolate pieces, optional

Dippers:
Sliced apples
Sliced pears
Cut-up banana
Large marshmallows
Yellow cake, cut into 1 1/2-inch cubes

Yield: 6 Servings

In medium glass bowl, combine caramels, coffee, milk and chocolate. Cook at **MEDIUM** 5 to 6 minutes; stir until smooth. Serve with assorted Dippers. If Fondue cools, reheat at **HIGH** 1 1/2 to 2 1/2 minutes.

BANANA SPLIT TOPPING

1 can (8 1/4 oz.) chunk pineapple, drained; reserve syrup
1 can (17 oz.) dark sweet pitted cherries in heavy syrup, drained; reserve syrup
1 1/2 tablespoons cornstarch
2 bananas, cut into 1-inch pieces
Ice Cream

Yield: 3 Cups

Set aside 1/4 cup reserved syrup. In 4-cup glass measure, combine remaining reserved syrup, pineapple and cherries. Cook at **HIGH** 4 to 5 minutes; stir occasionally. Blend cornstarch with remaining 1/4 cup syrup; stir until smooth. Stir into topping. Cook at **HIGH** 2 to 3 minutes, or until thickened; stir occasionally. Cool slightly; slice bananas over ice cream and add topping.

SUPER CHOCOLATE FROSTING

3 squares (1 oz. ea.) semi-sweet chocolate
1 can (14 oz.) sweetened condensed milk
1/2 teaspoon salt
1/2 teaspoon vanilla

Yield: 1 1/2 Cups

Place chocolate in medium bowl. Cook at **MEDIUM** 3 to 3 1/2 minutes, or until melted. Stir in milk and salt. Cook at **MEDIUM** 4 minutes; stir twice. Stir in vanilla. Cool completely before frosting cake.

BRANDIED CHERRY SAUCE

1 can (17 oz.) dark sweet pitted cherries in heavy syrup, drained; reserve syrup
Water
1/2 cup sugar
1 1/2 tablespoons cornstarch
1/4 cup brandy

Yield: 6 Servings

Reserve 1/4 cup syrup. To remaining syrup, add enough water to equal 1 1/4 cups. In medium bowl, combine syrup-water mixture, cherries and sugar. Cook at **HIGH** 3 to 4 minutes; stir once. Blend cornstarch with remaining 1/4 cup syrup; stir until smooth. Stir into sauce. Cook at **HIGH** 2 to 4 minutes, or until sauce is thickened; stir once. Transfer to serving dish.
In 1-cup glass measure, heat brandy at **HIGH** 1/2 to 3/4 minute. Pour over cherry sauce and carefully flame. Serve as desired, over vanilla ice cream, angel food cake or chocolate souffle.

HOT FUDGE SAUCE

4 squares (1 oz. ea.) unsweetened or semi-sweet chocolate
1 cup sugar
1 cup heavy cream
1/4 cup butter or margarine
1 tablespoon corn syrup
1 teaspoon vanilla

Yield: 2 Cups

In 2-quart glass bowl, combine chocolate, sugar, cream, butter and syrup. Cook at **HIGH** 9 to 11 minutes. Mixture will boil briskly; stir three times. Cool 15 minutes; stir in vanilla, until smooth and serve.

To reheat: *Heat 2 to 3 minutes, or until hot; stir once.*

CARAMEL CREAM FROSTING

8 caramels
1 1/2 to 2 tablespoons water, divided
1 package (3 oz.) cream cheese, softened
2 cups confectioners sugar

Yield: Frost Single Layer

Place caramels and 1 tablespoon water, in medium bowl. Cook at **HIGH** 2 to 3 minutes; stir until smooth. With electric mixer, blend in cream cheese, then sugar; add 1/2 to 1 tablespoon water to reach desired consistency.

BUTTERSCOTCH FUDGE

3 cups sugar
³/₄ cup butter or margarine
1 can (5¹/₃ oz.) evaporated milk
1 package (12 oz.) butterscotch flavored pieces
1 jar (7¹/₂ oz.) marshmallow cream
1 cup chopped walnuts
1 teaspoon vanilla

Yield: 3 Pounds

In 2¹/₂-quart casserole, combine sugar, butter and milk. Cook at **HIGH** 9 to 11 minutes, or until sugar is dissolved; stir twice. Add remaining ingredients and stir until butterscotch is melted. Turn into well greased oblong dish. Chill until firm; cut into squares to serve.

Variation:
*For **CHOCOLATE Fudge**, use 1 package (12 oz.) semi-sweet chocolate pieces for butterscotch.*

RAISIN CLUSTERS

8 squares (1 oz. ea.) semi-sweet chocolate
²/₃ cup sweetened condensed milk
1 cup raisins

Yield: 2 Dozen

Place chocolate in medium bowl. Cook at **MEDIUM** 3 to 3¹/₂ minutes, or until chocolate is melted. Add milk; stir until smooth. Stir in raisins. Drop by teaspoonful onto greased wax paper lined cookie sheet; chill.

Variations:
*For **ELEPHANT Clusters**, use 1 cup unsalted peanuts for raisins.*
*For **CHINESE Clusters**, use 1 cup crisp chow mein noodles.*

APPLE FUDGE BROWNIES

¹/₂ cup butter or margarine
2 squares (1 oz. ea.) unsweetened chocolate
1 cup packed brown sugar
¹/₂ cup applesauce
2 eggs
1 teaspoon vanilla
1 cup flour
¹/₂ teaspoon baking powder
¹/₄ teaspoon baking soda
1 cup chopped apple

Yield: 16 Brownies

Combine butter and chocolate in large glass bowl. Cook at **MEDIUM** 3 to 3¹/₂ minutes, or until melted. Stir in sugar, applesauce, eggs and vanilla. Gradually add flour, baking powder and soda; stir in apple. Pour in greased 8 or 9-inch square dish. Cook at **MEDIUM** 14 to 15 minutes, or until toothpick inserted near center comes out clean.
Let stand 10 minutes. Store, covered, until ready to serve.

QUICK BAR COOKIES (FROM MIX)

1 package (14 oz.) chocolate chip cookie mix
Ingredients as package directs

Yield: 16 Bars

Prepare mix according to package directions. Spread dough into ungreased 8 or 9-inch square dish. Cover with wax paper. Cook at **MEDIUM** 7 to 9 minutes, or until toothpick inserted near center comes out clean. Let stand, uncovered until cool. Store, covered, until ready to serve.

JAM BARS

1/4 cup butter or margarine, softened
1/4 cup sugar
1 egg
1/2 cup flour
1/4 cup chopped walnuts
1/2 teaspoon grated lemon peel
1/4 teaspoon cinnamon
1/8 teaspoon salt
1/2 cup raspberry or strawberry jam

Topping:
1/2 cup flour
1/4 cup packed brown sugar
3 tablespoons butter or margarine, softened

Yield: 16 Bars

Cream butter and sugar with electric mixer. Add egg flour, walnuts, lemon peel, cinnamon and salt. Mix well. Pat mixture into an 8-inch square dish. Cook at **HIGH** 3 to 4 minutes or until center is slightly firm.
Meanwhile, mix together topping ingredients until mixture resembles coarse crumbs. Spread jam on top of baked crust; sprinkle topping over jam. Cook at **HIGH** 3 to 5 minutes or until jam bubbles around edge.
Let stand until cool.

CRISPY MARSHMALLOW TREATS

1 package (10 oz.) marshmallows
1/4 cup butter or margarine
5 cups toasted rice cereal

Yield: 30 Squares

Place marshmallows and butter in large bowl. Cook at **HIGH** 4 to 5 minutes, or until marshmallows are completely melted; stir twice. Stir until smooth. Add cereal and stir to coat well. Press into greased oblong dish. Cool; cut into squares to serve.

Variation:
Stir in 1 cup salted peanuts or raisins with cereal.

MARBLE BROWNIES

1 package (22 1/2 to 23 3/4 oz.) fudge brownie mix
Ingredients as brownie package directs for fudge-type brownies
2 packages (3 oz. ea.) cream cheese
2 tablespoons butter or margarine
1 egg
1/4 cup sugar
1 tablespoon flour
1/2 teaspoon vanilla

Yield: 32 Brownies

Prepare fudge-type brownies according to package directions. Spread 1 cup batter into two greased 8 or 9-inch square dishes. Combine cream cheese and butter in small glass bowl. Cook at **MEDIUM** 1 1/2 to 2 1/2 minutes, or until softened; blend in remaining ingredients. Evenly divide cheese mixture into dishes; spoon remaining brownie batter on top. With knife, swirl gently to marble. Cover with wax paper. Cook at **LOW** 6 minutes and at **HIGH** 5 1/2 to 6 1/2 minutes, or until set. Repeat procedure with remaining dish.
Let stand, uncovered, until cool. Store, covered, until ready to serve.

NUTTY CHIP CHEWS

3/4 cup packed brown sugar
1/2 cup butter or margarine, softened
1 egg
1/4 cup milk
1 teaspoon vanilla
1 1/4 cups flour
1/2 teaspoon baking powder
1/2 cup chopped nuts
1 cup semi-sweet chocolate pieces

Yield: 16 Bars

Cream sugar and butter with electric mixer. Add egg, milk and vanilla. Stir in flour and baking powder until well blended; add nuts and 1/2 cup chocolate pieces. Spread batter into greased 8 or 9-inch square dish. Top with remaining chocolate. Cover with wax paper. Cook at **LOW** 6 minutes and at **HIGH** 4 to 5 minutes, or until toothpick inserted near center comes out clean. Let stand, uncovered, until cool. Store, covered, until ready to serve.

Custards and Puddings

COOKING PUDDING AND PIE FILLING MIXES

- Combine ingredients according to package directions.
- Use a glass container twice the volume of the mix.
- Stir twice during cooking time.
- Chill before serving (stir rice and tapioca pudding occasionally).

ITEM	APPROX. COOKING TIME at MEDIUM (in minutes)
Regular Pudding and Pie Filling 4 servings (3¹/₄ to 3³/₄ oz.) 6 servings (4³/₄ to 5¹/₂ oz.)	5 to 6 10 to 11
Egg Custard* (3 oz.)	8¹/₂ to 9¹/₂
Rice Pudding* (3³/₄ oz.)	8¹/₂ to 9¹/₂
Tapioca Pudding* (3¹/₂ oz.)	8¹/₂ to 9¹/₂

Mixture will thicken as it chills.

STEAMED DATE-NUT PUDDING

1¹/₄ cups flour
¹/₂ cup chopped walnuts
¹/₂ cup chopped dates
¹/₂ cup raisins
1 teaspoon cinnamon
¹/₂ teaspoon baking soda
¹/₂ teaspoon salt
³/₄ cup hot water
¹/₂ cup molasses
1 egg
2 tablespoons butter or margarine, melted

Yield: 12 Servings

In medium bowl, combine flour, walnuts, dates, raisins, cinnamon, baking soda and salt. Stir in water, molasses, egg and butter. Pour batter into a greased 10 to 12-cup fluted tube dish. Cover completely with plastic wrap. Cook at **MEDIUM** 7 to 9 minutes, or until pudding is set. Release plastic wrap.
Let stand, covered, 10 minutes. Invert onto serving platter; serve warm or cover until cool.

RAISIN BREAD PUDDING

2 cups milk
¹/₄ cup butter or margarine
5 eggs, beaten
1 cup sugar, divided
1 teaspoon vanilla
4 cups cubed raisin bread
¹/₈ teaspoon cinnamon

Yield: 6 Servings

Place milk and butter in 4-cup measure. Cook at **MEDIUM** 7 to 8 minutes, or until milk is scalded. Beat small amount of hot milk mixture into eggs. Beat eggs into rest of hot milk. Stir in ¹/₂ cup sugar and vanilla. Meanwhile, arrange bread cubes in 2-quart ring mold. Sprinkle with remaining sugar and cinnamon. Pour milk-egg mixture over bread. Cover with plastic wrap. Cook at **MEDIUM** 17 to 19 minutes, or until pudding is set.
Let stand 5 minutes. Serve warm or chilled.

BASIC EGG CUSTARD

1 1/2 cups milk
3 eggs, beaten
1/4 cup sugar
1/2 teaspoon vanilla
Dash nutmeg

Yield: 4 Servings

In 1-quart glass measure, heat milk at **MEDIUM** 4 1/2 to 5 1/2 minutes or until scalded; quickly stir in eggs, sugar and vanilla. Cook at **MEDIUM** 1 minute; stir twice. Pour into 4 greased custard cups (6 oz. ea.); sprinkle with nutmeg. Arrange cups in circular pattern in oven. Cook at **LOW** 6 1/2 to 7 minutes. Remove custards as they are cooked. Custards are cooked when they are firmly set about 1 inch from edge and center is thickened, but not set. Center will set as custard cools.

Variation:
*For **CARAMEL CUSTARD**, in small glass bowl, cook 1/2 cup sugar and 3 tablespoons water at **HIGH** 6 to 7 minutes or until sugar is melted and light brown. Pour into greased custard cups, tilting cups to coat bottom. Proceed as directed above.*

CHUNKY APPLESAUCE

3 pounds baking apples, peeled, cored and
    sliced (5 1/2 cups)
3/4 cup sugar or to taste
1/2 cup water
1/2 to 1 teaspoon cinnamon

Yield: 5 1/2 Cups

Combine all ingredients in large glass bowl. Cover with wax paper. Cook at **HIGH** 8 to 11 minutes, or until apples are soft; stir once. Mash apples until slightly chunky; serve warm or chilled.

BAKED APPLES

4 baking apples (6 oz. ea.)*
1/4 cup packed brown sugar
2 tablespoons finely chopped nuts or raisins
1/4 teaspoon cinnamon
2 tablespoons butter or margarine
1/4 cup water

Yield: 4 Servings

Core apples, leaving a small plug in blossom end; peel skin 1-inch from top. Combine sugar, nuts and cinnamon and fill each apple with mixture. Arrange apples in 8-inch square dish. Dot with butter; sprinkle with water. Cover with wax paper. Cook at **HIGH** 8 to 10 minutes. Let stand, 5 minutes before serving.

*Apples used in recipe are refrigerator cold; adjust timing for unchilled apples.

CHILLED CHOCOLATE ALMOND SOUFFLE

1 envelope unflavored gelatin
3/4 cup sugar, divided
3 eggs, separated
1 cup milk
2 squares (1 oz. ea.) unsweetened chocolate,
    melted
1/4 teaspoon almond extract
1 cup heavy cream, whipped
Slivered almonds
Whipped topping

Yield: 8 Servings

Mix gelatin and 1/2 cup sugar in large bowl. Beat egg yolks with milk; stir into gelatin. Cook at **MEDIUM** 5 to 5 1/2 minutes, or until gelatin is dissolved; stir occasionally. With wire whip, stir in chocolate and almond extract; chill until mixture mounds slightly.
Meanwhile, beat egg whites until soft peaks form; gradually add remaining sugar and beat until stiff. Fold in chocolate-almond mixture; fold in whipped cream. Turn into small souffle dish with 2-inch collar or 6-cup bowl and chill until firm. Garnish, if desired, with slivered almonds and additional whipped cream.

CURRIED FRUIT COMPOTE

1 can (17 oz.) apricot halves, drained;
   reserve syrup
1 can (16 oz.) peach slices, drained;
   reserve syrup
1/4 teaspoon curry powder
1/4 teaspoon cinnamon
1 tablespoon cornstarch
1/4 cup water
1/2 cup raisins

Yield: 6 Servings

In 2-cup glass measure, combine 1 cup reserved syrups, curry and cinnamon. Cook at **HIGH** 3 to 4 minutes. Blend cornstarch with water; stir until smooth. Stir into syrups. Cook at **HIGH** 2 to 3 minutes, or until slightly thickened; stir occasionally. In 8-inch square dish, combine apricots, peaches and raisins. Cook at **HIGH** 4 to 5 minutes; stir once. Pour in sauce. Cook at **HIGH** 1 to 2 minutes.
Let stand 5 minutes before serving.

CINNAMON PEARS WITH CARAMEL

4 large pears (6 oz. ea.)
1 tablespoon sugar
Dash cinnamon
1/4 cup water
25 caramels (about 7 1/2 oz.)
2 tablespoons butter or margarine
1 tablespoon rum, optional
1 tablespoon water
1/2 teaspoon cinnamon
Sweetened whipped cream

Yield: 4 Servings

Core pears and peel skin 1-inch from top. Combine sugar and dash cinnamon; sprinkle inside pears. Arrange pears in 8-inch square dish. Sprinkle with water. Cover with plastic wrap. Cook at **HIGH** 7 to 9 minutes, or until pears are tender; cool or chill.
Just before serving, in glass bowl, combine caramels, butter, rum, water and cinnamon. Cook at **HIGH** 2 1/2 to 4 minutes; stir until smooth.
In individual serving dishes, spoon sauce over pears; top with whipped cream.

FRUIT COBBLER

Filling:
2 cans (30 oz. ea.) peach slices or other
   canned fruit, drained; reserve 1/4 cup syrup
3 tablespoons flour
1/2 teaspoon lemon juice
1/2 teaspoon vanilla
1/2 teaspoon cinnamon

Topping:
1 cup buttermilk biscuit mix
1/4 cup packed brown sugar
1/4 cup butter or margarine, softened
2 tablespoons hot water

Yield: 6 Servings

In 8-inch dish, combine Filling ingredients, and reserved syrup. In bowl, combine Topping ingredients, stirring until combined.
Gently spread topping onto filling (topping will spread slightly when cooked). Sprinkle, if desired, with additional cinnamon, Cook at **HIGH** 14 to 16 minutes, or until topping is set. Let stand until cool.

Variations:
*For **FRESH PEACH** Cobbler, combine 1 1/2 pounds peaches, peeled and sliced, and 1/4 to 1/3 cup packed brown sugar. Cover with plastic wrap. Cook at **HIGH** 4 to 5 minutes or until tender. Follow above procedure, omitting 1/4 cup reserved syrup. For **QUICK FRUIT** Cobbler, substitute 2 cans (21 oz. ea.) fruit pie filling and 1/4 cup water for Filling ingredients.*

Pies

PREPARING PIE CRUSTS

- Prepare pastry according to recipe or package directions.
- If desired, for a single crust scratch pastry recipe, substitute 1/2 cup whole wheat flour for 1/2 cup all-purpose flour.
- Microwave pie crusts are light in color. A few drops of yellow food coloring may be mixed with the liquid before adding liquid to the flour mixture. This will give the crust a pale yellow color.
- Roll dough out and gently place in pie plate.
- Trim edge so a 3/4-inch overhang remains. Roll overhang down to rim of pie plate. Flute edge.
- Prick bottom and sides of pastry with fork.
- Let pie crust rest 10 minutes. The rest time helps reduce shrinkage.
- If desired, brush with dark corn syrup or molasses for sweet fillings, or brush with Worcestershire or soy sauce for savory fillings.
- For frozen crust, remove from foil pie plate and place in an 8 or 9-inch glass pie plate. Cook at **HIGH** 1/2 minute, then prick crust and, if desired, brush with dark corn syrup, molasses, Worcestershire or soy sauce.
- For crumb crusts combine 1/3 cup butter and 1/4 cup sugar in glass bowl. Cook until butter is melted. Combine 1 1/4 cup crumbs (graham crackers, chocolate or vanilla wafers). Firmly pat into 9-inch pie plate.
- Cook according to directions given in chart.
- Visually check for doneness. Pastry crusts should be opaque. If crust is undercooked, add cooking time in 15 second increments.
- Let stand until cool. Chill crumb crusts.

ITEM	POWER	APPROX. COOKING TIME (in minutes)
From Scratch or Mix	HIGH	5 to 6
Frozen	HIGH	4 1/2 to 5 1/2
Graham Cracker or Cookie Crumb	MEDIUM	3 to 3 1/2

FRESH PEACH PIE

2 pounds fresh peaches, peeled and sliced
1/2 cup packed brown sugar
1/2 to 1 tablespoon cornstarch
2 teaspoons lemon juice
1/2 teaspoon cinnamon
9-inch pastry shell, baked (see page 97)

Crumb Topping:
1/2 cup flour
1/3 cup packed brown sugar
1/4 cup butter or margarine, softened
1/3 cup finely chopped nuts
1/4 teaspoon cinnamon

Yield: 8 Servings

Toss peaches with sugar, cornstarch, lemon juice and cinnamon; arrange in prepared shell. Cover with wax paper. Cook at **HIGH** 5 to 7 minutes, or until peaches are almost tender. Meanwhile, combine all Crumb Topping ingredients. Sprinkle pie with Crumb Topping. Cook at **HIGH** 5 to 6 minutes, or until topping is set.
Let stand until cool.

Variation: For Fresh Apple Pie, use 2 pounds apples for peaches.

GRASSHOPPER PIE

3 cups miniature marshmallows
1/2 cup milk or half 'n half
3 tablespoons creme de cocoa
3 tablespoons green creme de menthe
1 cup heavy cream, whipped
9-inch chocolate cookie crumb crust, baked (see page 97)

Yield: 8 Servings

Combine marshmallows and milk in large bowl. Cook at **MEDIUM** 3 1/2 to 4 minutes; stir until smooth. Stir in creme de cocoa and creme de menthe; chill until mixture mounds slightly. Stir occasionally. Fold in whipped cream and turn into prepared crust. Chill until firm.

COCONUT LEMON MERINGUE PIE

1½ cups sugar
⅓ cup cornstarch
¼ teaspoon salt
1½ cups boiling water
3 eggs, separated
½ cup lemon juice
3 tablespoons butter or margarine
Grated peel of 1 lemon
9-inch pie shell, baked (see page 97)
⅓ cup sugar
¼ cup toasted coconut (see page 102)

Yield: 8 Servings

In a 3-quart casserole, combine 1½ cups sugar, cornstarch and salt; stir in boiling water. Cover with lid. Cook at **HIGH** 9 to 10 minutes, or until thickened. Halfway through cooking, stir once. Stir in small amount of hot mixture into egg yolks; return to hot mixture, beating until well blended. Add lemon juice, butter and lemon peel. Pour into pie shell; set aside.
Meanwhile, beat egg whites until soft peaks form, gradually add remaining sugar and beat until stiff. Spread meringue over filling, making sure it touches crust all around. Sprinkle with coconut. Cook at **HIGH** 3 to 4 minutes, or until meringue is set. Cool completely.

PUMPKIN PIE

1 can (16 oz.) cooked pumpkin
1 cup evaporated milk
2 eggs
½ cup sugar
¼ cup packed brown sugar
½ teaspoon salt
1 teaspoon cinnamon
½ teaspoon ginger
¼ teaspoon cloves
9-inch pastry shell, baked (see page 97)

Yield: 8 Servings

Combine pumpkin, milk, eggs, sugars, salt and spices. Pour into prepared shell. Cook at **MEDIUM** 20 to 24 minutes, or until center is almost set.
Let stand, covered with wax paper, until cool.

ORANGE CHIFFON PIE

1 envelope unflavored gelatin
⅓ cup sugar
4 eggs, separated
1 can (11 oz.) mandarin orange sections, drained; reserve ⅔ cup syrup
2 tablespoons lemon juice
½ teaspoon grated lemon peel
½ cup sugar
9-inch graham cracker crumb crust, baked (see page 97)

Yield: 8 Servings

Mix gelatin and ⅓ cup sugar in medium glass bowl; stir in egg yolks blended with reserved syrup, lemon juice and lemon peel. Cook at **HIGH** 4½ to 5½ minutes, or until gelatin is dissolved; stir twice. Chill until mixture mounds slightly; stir occasionally.
Meanwhile, beat egg whites until soft peaks form; gradually add ½ cup sugar and beat until stiff. Fold in gelatin mixture and half of oranges; turn into prepared crust. Chill until firm; garnish with remaining oranges.

PECAN PIE

1 cup dark corn syrup
¼ cup packed brown sugar
3 eggs
2 tablespoons butter or margarine, melted
1 teaspoon vanilla
¾ cup chopped pecans
9-inch pastry shell, baked (see page 97)
Sweetened whipped cream

Yield: 8 Servings

Combine syrup, sugar, eggs, butter and vanilla; stir in pecans. Pour into prepared crust. Cook at **MEDIUM** 8 to 9 minutes, or until pie is set. Let stand until cool. Garnish with sweetened whipped cream.

HEATING FROZEN CONVENIENCE FOODS

ITEM	POWER	APPROX. COOKING TIME (in minutes)	SPECIAL HINTS
APPETIZERS Bite Size	HIGH	2 to 3	Heat 12 at a time on paper towel lined paper plate or microwave oven roasting rack. Brush pastry items with Worcestershire sauce.
MAIN DISH Frozen Dinner (6 to 11 oz.) (12 to 16 oz.) (17 to 21 oz.)	 HIGH HIGH HIGH	 4 to 8 6 to 8 11 to 13	Remove tray from box. Remove foil or plastic cover. Remove any cake-like desserts such as brownies; they may burn. Cover completely with plastic wrap.
Entrees (6 to 11 oz.) (12 to 16 oz.) (17 to 21 oz.)	 MEDIUM MEDIUM MEDIUM	 6 to 11 10 to 13 16 to 21	Remove from foil container and place in appropriately sized glass container. Cover with lid or cover completely with plastic wrap.
Breakfast Entree (4$\frac{1}{2}$ to 8 oz.)	HIGH	2$\frac{1}{2}$ to 4	Remove tray from box. Leave plastic film on breakfast. For breakfasts without film, cover completely with plastic film.
French Toast 2 pieces 4 pieces	MEDIUM	1$\frac{3}{4}$ to 2$\frac{1}{4}$ 4$\frac{1}{2}$ to 5	
Waffles 2 pieces 4 pieces	MEDIUM	1$\frac{3}{4}$ to 2$\frac{1}{4}$ 2$\frac{3}{4}$ to 3$\frac{1}{4}$	
Fried Chicken 2 pieces 4 pieces	HIGH	4$\frac{1}{2}$ to 6$\frac{1}{2}$ 9 to 11	Arrange on paper towel lined paper plate, cover with paper towel.
Fried Fish Fillets 2 fillets 4 fillets	HIGH	2 to 4 4 to 6	
Fish Cakes 4 cakes	HIGH	3$\frac{1}{2}$ to 4$\frac{1}{2}$	Arrange on microwave oven roasting rack.
Pouch Entrees Single Pouch (4 to 11 oz.) Double Pouch (8 to 11 oz.)	HIGH	 3$\frac{1}{2}$ to 7 5 to 7	Pierce 1 hole in each pouch. Place on paper plate or glass dish. Double pouch entrees should be placed side by side.

ITEM	POWER	APPROX. COOKING TIME (in minutes)	SPECIAL HINTS

BAKED GOODS
  Brownies (13 oz.)
  Cupcakes (6)
  (10 to 11 oz.)
  Cheese Cake (17 oz.)
  Layer Cakes
  (17 to 18 oz.)
  Pound Cake (10¾ oz.)
  Coffee Cake
  (11 to 12 oz.)
	DEFROST	4 to 6
		3 to 5
		
		7 to 9
		3 to 5
		
		2 to 4
		6 to 8
			Remove from original container; arrange on serving plate.
			
			Add an additional 1 to 1½ minutes to serve warm.

BAGELS
  2
  4
DANISH
  1
  2
  4 (9 oz. package)
Dinner Rolls (6)
Donuts
  Plain or Sugar coated
  1
  2
  4
Hard Rolls
(1 to 1¼ oz. ea.)
  1
  2
  4
	DEFROST
	
	DEFROST
	
	DEFROST
	DEFROST
	
	DEFROST
		
		4 to 6
		6 to 8
		
		1 to 2
		3 to 4
		5 to 7
		3 to 5
		
		1½ to 2
		2 to 5
		5 to 6
		
		1 to 1½
		2 to 3
		4 to 5
			Each individually wrapped in a paper towel (for 1 or 2). Arrange on paper plate; cover with paper towel (for 4 or 6).

MISCELLANEOUS
(TO THAW)
Frozen Juice Concentrates
  (6 oz.)
  (12 oz.)
Non-Dairy Creamer
  (16 oz.)
Pancake/Muffin Batter
  (10 oz.)
Whipped Topping
  (9 oz.)
Frozen Mixed Fruit
  (10 oz.)
 	
Frozen Vegetables
  (6 oz.)
  (10 oz.)
	
	MEDIUM
	
	DEFROST
	
	DEFROST
	
	DEFROST
	
	DEFROST
	
	DEFROST
		
		¾ to 1¼
		1½ to 2½
		
		9 to 10
		
		9 to 10
		
		3 to 5
		
		9 to 10
		
		6 to 8
		10 to 12
			Remove lid. If container is foil lined, remove to pitcher.
			
			Open carton.
			
			Open carton.
			
			Heat in original plastic tub.
			
			Pierce pouch or remove metal lid; set on saucer.
			Pierce box; set on saucer. If box is foil wrapped, remove foil. If vegetables are in pouch, pierce pouch.

COOKING CANNED FOODS

- Empty contents of can into serving dish.
- Cook, covered, at **HIGH**→stand
- Stir, occasionally during cooking.

ITEM	APPROXIMATE COOKING TIME (in minutes) at HIGH	STAND TIME (in minutes)
Baked Beans (8 oz.) (15 to 16 oz.)	$1^1/_2$ to $2^1/_2$ $3^1/_2$ to $4^1/_2$	3 3
Chow Mein (15 to 16 oz.)	3 to 4	3
Corned Beef Hash (15 oz.)	3 to 4	3
Macaroni and Cheese (15 oz.)	4 to 5	3
Sloppy Joe (15 oz.)	$4^1/_2$ to $5^1/_2$	3
Ravioli (15 oz.)	4 to 5	3
Vegetables (8 oz.) (16 oz.)	2 to 3 3 to 4	3 3

QUICK TIPS

To further illustrate the versatility of your microwave oven, here are some of our favorite tips to help you save more time, even when doing the little things. Because all times given are approximate and may vary, do not leave oven unattended.

- SOFTEN CREAM CHEESE, cheese spread or a stick of BUTTER. At LOW a 3 oz. package of cream cheese or ¼ pound of butter will be spreadable in ½ to 1 minute.
- FRESHEN a STALE ROLL. Wrap in wax paper or paper napkin and heat at MEDIUM about ¼ to ½ minute.
- HEAT PANCAKE and other SYRUPS. Heat at HIGH in a glass pitcher for 1 to 2 minutes (depending upon quantity).
- HEAT CITRUS FRUITS at MEDIUM ½ to 1 minute. They will be easier to squeeze, giving you more juice.
- DRY LEMON and ORANGE PEELS in your microwave oven for your own bottled grated peel. Place grated peel in small glass bowl. Heat at HIGH ½ to 1 minute or until dry; stir once.
- REMOVE OVEN ODORS easily. Combine water with the juice and peel of a lemon in a small glass bowl. Heat at HIGH 5 minutes; wipe oven interior with damp cloth.
- Have FRESH COFFEE all day. Refrigerate what is not used at breakfast. Reheat by the mugful at HIGH 1½ to 2 minutes.
- REHEAT COLD FRUIT PIE at MEDIUM ½ to 1 minute for fresh from the oven flavor.
- DRY HERBS quickly in your microwave oven. Place a few springs or ½ cup leaves between paper towels and heat at HIGH 1 to 1½ minutes or until dry and crumbly. Timings may vary with different herbs.
- For CAREFREE BARBECUES, partially cook chicken, ribs, etc. in the microwave oven. Season and finish on the grill.
- QUICK COOK CHICKEN pieces at HIGH when you need cut-up, cooked chicken for salads, sandwiches or casseroles.
- SEPARATE COLD BACON slices easily. Heat package at HIGH ¼ to ½ minute.
- Heat LIQUEURS for FLAMING DESSERTS in a glass measure at HIGH 15 to 30 seconds. Pour over dessert and ignite.
- SOFTEN HARD ICE CREAM for serving or molding at LOW. Heat ½ gallon, 3½ to 5 minutes.
- DRY BREAD for croutons or bread crumbs. Two cups bread cubes, in shallow glass dish will dry in 3 to 4 minutes, at HIGH; stir occasionally.
- BLANCH NUTS by heating in boiling water at HIGH ½ to 1 minute. Drain and slip skins off by rubbing between paper towel.
- SOFTEN DRY FRUIT. In small glass bowl, sprinkle fruit with water and heat, covered, with plastic wrap at HIGH ½ to ¾ minute.
- SOFTEN HARD BROWN SUGAR. In glass dish, place sugar and slice of fresh bread or apple wedge; cover and heat at HIGH. One cup sugar will soften in ½ to 1 minute.
- MELT BUTTER or CHOCOLATE for cooking. Heat butter (¼ lb.) at LOW 2½ to 3½ minutes and chocolate (1 oz.) 2½ to 3 minutes at MEDIUM. Chocolate will not lose its shape when melted, so check before adding extra time.
- Toast COCONUT easily at HIGH. In 9-inch glass pie plate, heat ⅓ cup for 2 to 2½ minutes, or until golden brown; stir twice.
- Roast NUTS quickly at HIGH. In small glass bowl, heat 1½ cups for 3 to 4 minutes; stir twice.
- Toast SESAME SEEDS at HIGH. In small glass bowl, heat ¼ cup for 2½ to 3½ minutes; stir twice.

Y10AP
(84•6)
Printed in Japan